Socialism: utopian and scientific

Socialism: utopian and scientific
Frederick Engels

Bookmarks
London, Chicago, Melbourne

Socialism: utopian and scientific / *Frederick Engels*
This edition published May 1993
Bookmarks, 265 Seven Sisters Road, London N4 2DE
Bookmarks, PO Box 16085, Chicago, Il. 60616
Bookmarks, GPO Box 1473N, Melbourne 3001
ISBN 0 906224 85 3
Printed by Cox and Wyman Ltd, Reading, England

Bookmarks is linked to an international grouping of socialist
organisations:
AUSTRALIA: **International Socialist Organisation**,
GPO Box 1473N, Melbourne 3001
BELGIUM: **Socialisme International**,
Rue Lovinfosse 60, 4030 Grevignée
BRITAIN: **Socialist Workers Party**,
PO Box 82, London E3 3LH
CANADA: **International Socialists**,
PO Box 339, Station E, Toronto, Ontario M6H 4E3
CYPRUS: **Workers Democracy**,
PO Box 7280, Nicosia, Cyprus
DENMARK: **Internationale Socialister**,
Ryesgade 8, 3, 8000, Århus C
FRANCE: **Socialisme International**,
BP 189, 75926 Paris, Cedex 19
GERMANY: **Sozialistische Arbeitersgruppe**,
Wolfsgangstrasse 81, W-6000, Frankfurt 1
GREECE: **Organosi Sosialistiki Epanastasi**,
PO Box 8161, 10010, Omonia, Athens
HOLLAND: **Groep Internationale Socialisten**,
PO Box 9720, 3506 GR Utrecht
IRELAND: **Socialist Workers Movement**,
PO Box 1648, Dublin 8
NEW ZEALAND: **International Socialist Organisation**,
PO Box 6157, Dunedin
NORWAY: **Internasjonale Sosialister**,
Postboks 9226, Grønland 0134, Oslo
POLAND: **Solidarnosc Socjalistyczna**,
PO Box 12, 01-900 Warszawa 118
SOUTH AFRICA: **International Socialists of South Africa**,
PO Box 18530, Hillbrow 2038
UNITED STATES: **International Socialist Organisation**,
PO Box 16085, Chicago, Il. 60616

Contents

This booklet was written between January and March 1880. It is taken from a number of chapters of Engels' larger work, *Anti Dühring*.

Introduction

THIS IS a startling book, especially for those reading these pages for the first time. Although it was intended as a popular pamphlet, Frederick Engels' work is much more than a simple condemnation of the evils of capitalism as it appeared in 1880. Such a pamphlet would have dated very quickly. The secret of the continuing relevance of *Socialism: utopian and scientific* is its deeply historical structure. The account of the crisis of feudalism and the emergence of the capitalist class and the working class from the old agricultural and urban guild structures of mediaeval Europe is so expertly and concisely handled that repetition here is pointless. But there are a series of issues with which Engels deals that are, nevertheless, worth highlighting.

The first is the specific attention which Engels pays to the development of capitalism in England. His 'Introduction to the first English Edition' substantially adds to the passages in the main body of the book. After a few pages discussing the circumstances in which he came to write *Socialism: utopian and scientific* and some passages discussing the emergence of materialist ideas in England after the revolution of the 1640s, Engels launches into one of the best concise accounts of the development of capitalism in England available anywhere, carefully tracing the political and institutional changes which accompanied the English bourgeoisie's ascent to power from the English revolution to the parliamentary reform acts of the nineteenth century.

The second notable point about *Socialism: utopian and scientific* is the care with which it treats the battle of ideas which accompanied the emergence of capitalism. At every point Engels is an accurate and sensitive observer of the ideological scene—whether it be the emergence of rational, scientific ideas as a challenge to religious mysticism during the eighteenth century Enlightenment, or the importance of Calvin's Protestant individualism in revolt against the ideological fortress of feudalism, the Catholic church, or the English bourgeoisie's first heroic embrace of science after the English Revolution and its subsequent retreat into shame-faced religion in order to better control the new working class. Finally, Engels surveys the battle for socialist ideas among the new working class. This concern with ideas can only come as another surprise to those who only know of the theories of Engels and Karl Marx from their critics. Marxism, after all, is often said to be crudely economistic and therefore unable to account for how ideas change and develop. Nothing, as even the briefest acquaintance with these passages in *Socialism: utopian and scientific* will show, could be further from the truth.

What Engels would not countenance, however, is a radical separation of the social and economic conditions under which people live their lives and the ideas which they hold about those lives. Yet it is just this which Engels' latter day critics would like to force upon contemporary Marxists. The importance of Engels' approach comes through strongly in the passages in which he describes the fundamental features of the capitalist system as it emerged from its long historical development. In this Engels proves that his powers of analysis are as great as his powers of historical description. He captures the two fundamental divisions which make a society capitalist: 'on the one hand... the class antagonisms prevailing in modern society between proprietors and non-proprietors, between capitalists and wage workers, and on the other... the anarchy ruling in production.'

Here Engels isolates the two interlocking contradictions which have governed the development of the capitalist system from its beginnings through Engels' time to our own. The uncontrolled competition for profit between the different capitalist enterprises, the 'anarchy ruling in production', ensures that the struggle between the classes—over the length of the working day, over the productivity of labour and thus over jobs and wages—is an endemic, not accidental, feature of the system. And the same planless pursuit of profit also produces economic crises where although 'means of production, means of subsistence, available workers, all the elements of production and of general wealth are there in abundance' they lie idle because 'in capitalist society the means of production cannot begin to function unless they have first been converted into capital, into the means for exploitation of human labour power'. The need for the capitalists to turn a profit 'stands like a ghost' between the workers and the means for their subsistence. In this respect at least the last years of the twentieth century appear very like the last years of the nineteenth century.

But for all the similarities that modern capitalism shares with its previous incarnations, Engels would have been the last to claim that the system remained the same as it aged. One significant change is foreshadowed in Engels' discussion of the Marxist attitude to state ownership of industry. Again, those who have heard left wing Labour Party members argue that nationalisation is inherently socialist, or listened to those who believed that the Stalinist states in Eastern Europe were socialist because the state controlled the economy, will be surprised.

Engels' historical perspective allows him to show how competition between different capitalist firms led to the bankruptcy of the least profitable, the growth of the more profitable, to merger and takeover and, as an inevitable result, to the rise of joint stock companies, trusts and monopolies. Finally, as part of the same process, the state is forced to take a hand in the direct management of the economy. But, Engels insists, this does not make the state a 'socialist state': 'The modern state, whatever its form, is an essentially capitalist machine, the state of the capitalists, the ideal aggregate capitalist. The more productive forces it takes over into its possession, the more it becomes a real aggregate capitalist, the more citizens it exploits. The workers remain wage workers, proletarians. The capitalist relationship is not abolished, rather it is pushed to the limit.'

If carrying out nationalisation alone were enough to define a socialist, jokes Engels, then Bismarck's nationalisation of the Prussian railways would make him a socialist, Napoleon and Metternich's nationalisation of the tobacco trade would make them socialists and 'the Royal Maritime Company, the Royal Porcelain Manufacture, and even the regimental tailors in the army would be socialist institutions'.

So long as class society exists the state will remain a mechanism for the 'forcible holding down of the exploited class in conditions of oppression (slavery, villeinage or serfdom, wage labour) given by the existing mode of production.' Only when the rule of the old order, both in its economic and political aspects, has been broken in a revolution can workers begin to run society for themselves, along lines that they themselves decide. In the first instance they will create their own state, but a state radically different from any that has gone before—a democratic state in which, for the first time since the pre-history of humanity, the majority democratically control the political realm because they also control the social and economic realm.

But even this state will not last long: 'As soon as there is no class to be held in subjection any longer, as soon as class domination and the struggle for individual existence based on anarchy of production existing up to now are eliminated... there is nothing left to repress, nothing necessitating a special repressive force, a state. The first act in which that state really comes forward as the representative of the whole of society—the taking possession of the means of production in the name of society— is at the same time its last independent act as a state.' And so Engels concludes, in a phrase that has become famous as a definition of a socialist society, 'The interference of the state power in social relations become superfluous in one sphere after another, and then it dies away of itself. The government of persons is replaced by the administration of things and the direction of the processes of production. The state is not abolished, *it withers away.*'

Engels' clarity on the question of state ownership is a function of the fact that, by 1880, many of the trends that were to become so marked in twentieth century capitalism were already visible. Nationalisation was one outgrowth of the process of competition; the recruitment of a layer of salaried managers by the capitalists themselves was another. This phenomenon, highlighted by myriad twentieth century sociologists as proof that capitalism has changed its spots, had a rather different significance for Engels. For him it was proof that the older the system becomes the more the collective and social nature of production conflicts with the private ownership of the means of production, forcing even the capitalists to delegate some of their functions to a social layer which was *with* them but not *of* them, shared their interests but was not identical with them. This development really showed that the capitalist class had become superfluous, could be 'dispensed with' since 'all the social functions of the capitalist are now conducted by salaried employees.'

Ironically, perhaps the only passages in *Socialism: utopian and scientific* which appear dated are those which refer to the utopian socialists of the title. Engels explains the conditions under which utopian socialism arose as the period between the end of the great French Revolution and the emergence of an organised and independent working class movement in the 1830s. During that transitory period the working class was still forming itself amidst the great mass of propertyless poor created by the final decomposition of the feudal system and the emergence of the capitalist system. At this time 'the proletariat, which was only just separating itself from these propertyless masses as the nucleus of a new class and was as yet quite incapable of independent political action, appeared as an oppressed, suffering estate, to which, in its incapacity to help itself, help could at best be brought from without, from above down.'

To this practical situation the utopian socialists brought ideas forged by an encounter with the philosophers of the Enlightenment. If society presented nothing but abuses then 'to remove them was the task of reason. It was a question of inventing a new more perfect social order and of imposing it on society from without, by propaganda and wherever possible by the example of model experiments.' Before trade unions, before general strikes and workers' insurrections, before workers' councils—that is before the idea of workers' self emancipation formed the heart of Marxism—and with the whole Enlightenment tradition as the only intellectual weapon to hand all this was the unavoidable starting point of the socialist movement. By the 1830s and 1840s ideas began to change. But before ideas changed, reality changed. 'In the beginning', as Engels notes, 'was the deed'. And in this case the deeds were those of workers in struggle: 'In 1831, the first working class rising took place in Lyons; between 1838 and 1842, the first national working class movement, that of the English Chartists, reached its height. The class struggle between proletariat and bourgeoisie came to the front in the history of the most advanced countries in Europe'. But after nearly 150 years of such struggles, surely a critique of such primitive notions is of little use to socialists today.

This is not the case. Utopian socialist politics are still with us, though they have been regenerated in very different conditions to those which gave birth to the first utopians. Then they were a product of the absolute immaturity of the working class, but modern day utopians are a product of defeat and demoralisation in the working class movement. Both share the touchstone of utopianism: the belief that workers themselves cannot or will not fight for socialism and that it will therefore have to be imposed from above. The late 1970s and 1980s in Britain, as in the United States and much of Europe, was a period of retreat for the workers' movement. From the Meriden motorcycle co-operative and the Lucas Plan for alternative production, to the peace camps of the Greenham Common women and feminist consciousness raising circles, from the experiments of the Greater London Council under Ken Livingstone to the pacifism of the Campaign for Nuclear Disarmament, a new utopianism ran through the movement. Where, in the aftermath of the upheavals of 1968 and in the midst of the class struggles of the early 1970s, concentration on workers' self activity had resulted in the rebirth of a genuine, if minority, revolutionary tradition, now the ebbing of the struggle gave birth to a thousand recipes and blueprints, few of which arose from, or had any lasting influence on, the day to day struggles of workers. Some, like the Greenham women and much of the feminist movement generally, deliberately counterposed their schemes for change to the socialist tradition.

Inevitably all these trends were linked to the Labour Party, the modern home of philanthropic reformers. Utopianism and gradual reformism may seem like strange bedfellows, but their common

14

ground is a disbelief in the independent power of workers themselves to overthrow the system. The complementary creed holds that well meaning reformers must therefore perform the task by using propaganda and 'the example of model experiments' to convince the establishment of the virtue and reasonableness of socialism. Every dull reformist harbours a utopian illusion in his heart, like the workaday clerk day-dreaming romantic fancies at their desk. There is just one vital difference between the first utopians and their latter day, and mostly unconscious, imitators. The first utopians were praised by Engels as heroic figures, daring to think ahead of their time and wishing for a genuine revolution in the way society was ordered. Modern day utopians, for all the grandeur of their plans, fall far below that which history has already shown the workers' movement to be capable of. They consciously oppose themselves to the revolutionary potential of the working class, whereas the first utopians acted through unavoidable ignorance of the real possibilities.

The final surprise in these pages is that, in a brief pamphlet, Engels spends a great deal of time discussing questions of method and philosophy. He clearly felt that no introduction to Marxism would be complete unless its readers could gain from it a clear idea of how the Marxist method differed from bourgeois philosophy.

Engels is careful to distinguish historical materialism from two rival conceptions. One was the idealist tradition, originating in France but finding its most representative figures in the German philosophers Kant and Hegel who, in different ways, insisted that human thought was the motive force in history. The other was the materialist tradition which arose in Britain as a result of the seventeenth century revolution, and the scientific revolution which accompanied it, and flourished in eighteenth century Enlightenment France, reaching its peak with the outbreak of the French Revolution in 1789. This materialism reduced thought to a passive reflection of the world, robbing it of any active part in changing the world. Engels is a generous critic, paying tribute to both these pre-socialist trends of thought. But he is nonetheless insistent that they both represent partial truths.

The first, idealist, trend misses the fact that thoughts are ultimately 'the more or less abstract images of actual things and processes' and so were subject to change as historical circumstances changed. Thus the role of thought in human history is, in Engels' view, a product of the fact that 'human history is a process of development, which, by its very nature, cannot find its intellectual final term in the discovery of any so-called absolute truth.' From religion to the stock objection that human nature is a barrier to socialism such arguments are still heard today. History, on these accounts, is simply the working out of certain predetermined patterns—in our minds, our genes, our soul—'existing somehow from eternity before the world existed'.

The second, materialist, trend misses the point that thought does not simply reflect the world, it reacts upon it by guiding our actions. Indeed, Engels is insistent that the only way in which we can judge the correctness or otherwise of our views about the world is by engaging in action which seeks to change the world. There is no other ultimate criteria.

16

In place of these two equally misconceived alternatives Engels gives a brilliant outline of the Marxist dialectic. It had been, Engels argues, 'the greatest merit' of the Hegelian system that 'the whole world, natural, historical, intellectual, is for the first time represented as a process, ie, as in constant motion, change, transformation, development; and the attempt was made to show internal connections in this motion and development. From this point of view the history of mankind no longer appeared as a wild whirl of senseless deeds of violence, all equally condemnable at the judgement seat of mature philosophic reason and best forgotten as quickly as possible, but the process of the evolution of humanity itself.'

Any non-dialectical theory will fail to see the connections between the different aspects of the totality of human existence, fail to see the contradictions between the different elements of that totality which ensure that struggle and conflict result in change and development, not stability and quietism. Idealism breeds passivity by insisting that all we need to do is transform our thinking and the world will follow suit. Crude materialism ends in the same result by arguing that if we just wait on the world to change then peoples' thinking will reflect those changes sooner or later. Non-dialectical theory, or metaphysical thinking to use Engels' term, may produce very valuable results in specialised fields but it 'inevitably bumps into a limit sooner or later, beyond which it becomes one sided, restricted, abstract, lost in insoluble contradictions, because in the presence of individual things it forgets their connections; because in the presence of their existence it forgets

17

their coming into being and passing away; because in their state of rest it forgets their motion.' But dialectics 'grasps things and their conceptual images essentially in their interconnection, in their concatenation, their motion, their coming into and passing out of existence.' Engels' whole analysis of the decomposition of feudalism and the rise of capitalism is a perfect example of such a dialectical analysis, combining an understanding of the fact that human beings can make their own history with an equally clear comprehension of the limits and possibilities imposed on such change by the material circumstances under which it takes place.

Very few authors manage to combine a clear, uncluttered, accessible writing style with deep insight into how society works and a comprehensive historical analysis of its development. Fewer still manage to combine both with brevity. Frederick Engels, perhaps even more than Karl Marx, was one who did. It is not surprising then that when Engels' *Socialism: utopian and scientific* was first published it was even more popular than the *Communist Manifesto* as an introduction to revolutionary socialism.

John Rees
March 1993

Foreword to the first French Edition

THE PAGES included in this brochure, first published in the form of three articles in the *Revue socialiste*, have been selected and translated from Frederick Engels' latest work *Revolution in Science*.[1]

Frederick Engels, one of the most outstanding representatives of modern socialism, came to people's attention in 1844 for his 'Outline of a Critique of Political Economy', which first appeared in the *Deutsch-Französische Jahrbücher* published by Marx and Ruge in Paris.[2] In the 'Outline' some general principles of scientific socialism were already formulated. In Manchester, where he was living at the time, Engels wrote in German *The Condition of the Working Class in England* (1845), an important work to which Marx pays a deserved tribute in his *Capital*. During his first stay in England, and also later from Brussels, he contributed to the *Northern Star*, the official organ of the socialist movement, and to Robert Owen's *New Moral World*.

During his stay in Brussels, he and Marx founded the Communist Association of German Workers, which was in touch with the Flemish and Waloon workers' clubs; and together with Bornstedt, they founded the *Deutsche-Brüsseler-Zeitung*.[3] On the invitation of its German Committee (resident in London), they joined the League of the Just, which was originally founded by Karl Schapper after he was forced to flee from France for his part in the Blanqui conspiracy in 1839. Thereafter the League, ridding itself of the traditional form of a secret society, was reorganised into the international Communist League. Nevertheless, under the prevailing circumstances the League had to be kept secret from the governments. In 1847, at the International Congress called by the League in London, Marx and Engels were commissioned to draw up the *Manifesto of the Communist Party*, which was published shortly before the February Revolution and translated almost immediately into all the European languages.

In the same year they worked for the establishment of the Brussels Democratic Association, an international open society where the representatives of bourgeois radicals rubbed shoulders with socialist workers.

After the February Revolution, Engels became one of the editors of the *Neue Rheinische Zeitung*, which was founded by Marx in 1848 at Cologne and was banned in May 1849 because of a coup d'etat in Prussia.[4] After Engels had taken part in the Elberfeld insurrection, he went through the Campaign of Baden launched against the Prussians (June-July 1849) as adjutant to Willich, then the colonel of one of the volunteer battalions.

In London, in 1850, he contributed to the *Neue Rheinische Zeitung. Politisch-ökonomische Revue*, published by Marx and printed in Hamburg.[5] In it Engels first published 'The Peasant War in Germany', which appeared 19 years later as a pamphlet in Leipzig and went through three editions.

After the revival of the socialist movement in

Germany, Engels contributed to the *Volksstaat* and to *Vorwärts*, writing the most important articles which appeared in them, most of which were later reprinted in pamphlet form: *On Social Relations in Russia, Prussian Spirits in the German Reichstag, On the Housing Question, The Bakuninists in Action*, etc.[6]

After Engels moved from Manchester to London in 1870, he became a member of the General Council of the International, and was put in charge of correspondence with Spain, Portugal and Italy.

The series of articles which he sent to *Vorwärts* recently and ironically entitled *Herr Eugen Dühring's Revolution in Science*, is an answer to the allegedly new theories of Herr Eugen Dühring on science in general and on socialism in particular. This series then came out in one volume and was a great success among German socialists. In this pamphlet we present the extract which best characterises the theoretical part of the book, and which constitutes what may be called an *introduction to scientific socialism*.

Karl Marx
May 1880

Preface to the first German edition

THE FOLLOWING work is taken from three chapters of my book, *Herr Eugen Dühring's Revolution in Science*, Leipzig, 1878. I put it together for my friend Paul Lafargue for translation into French and added a few extra remarks. The French translation revised by me appeared first in the *Revue socialiste* and then independently under the title, *Socialisme utopique et socialisme scientifique*, Paris, 1880. A rendering into Polish made from the French translation has just appeared in Geneva and bears the title, *Socyjalizm utopijny a naukowy*, Imprimerie de l'Aurore, Geneva, 1882.

The surprising success of the Lafargue translation in the French speaking countries, and especially in France itself, forced me to consider whether a separate German edition of these three chapters would not likewise be of value. Then the editors of the Zurich *Sozialdemokrat*[1] informed me that a demand was generally being raised within the German Social Democratic Party for the publication of new propaganda pamphlets, and they asked me whether I would not apply those three chapters to this purpose. Naturally, I agreed and put my work at their disposal.

It was, however, not originally written for immediate popular propaganda. How could what was in the first place a purely scientific work be suitable for that? What changes in form and content were required?

So far as form is concerned, only the many foreign words could arouse doubts. But even Lassalle in his speeches and propaganda writings was not at all sparing of foreign words and to my knowledge there has been no complaint about it. Since that time our workers have read newspapers to a far greater extent and far more regularly and have to that degree become more familiar with foreign words. I have restricted myself to removing all unnecessary foreign words. For those that were unavoidable I have refrained from adding so-called explanatory translations. The unavoidable foreign words, for the most part generally accepted scientific-technical expressions, would not have been unavoidable if they had been translatable. Translation, therefore, distorts the sense; it confuses instead of explaining. Here oral information is much more helpful.

On the other hand, I think I can assert that the content will give German workers few difficulties. In general, only the third section is difficult, but far less so for workers, whose general conditions of life it concerns, than for the 'educated' bourgeois. In the many explanatory additions I have made here, I have had in mind not so much the workers as the 'educated' readers—persons of the type of Deputy von Eynern, *Geheimrat* Heinrich von Sybel and other Treitschkes,[2] who are governed by the irresistible impulse to demonstrate again and again in black and white their frightful ignorance and their consequently understandable colossal misconception of socialism. If Don Quixote tilts his lance at windmills, that is in keeping with his job and his role; but we cannot possibly allow Sancho Panza anything of the sort.

Such readers will also be surprised to encounter the Kant-Laplace cosmogony, modern natural science and Darwin, classical German philosophy and Hegel in a sketch of the history of the development of socialism. But scientific socialism is indeed an essentially German product and could arise only in that nation whose classical philosophy had kept alive the tradition of conscious dialectics: in Germany.[3] The materialist conception of history and its special application to the modern class struggle between the proletariat and the bourgeoisie was only possible through the mediation of dialectics. And if the schoolmasters of the German bourgeoisie have drowned the memory of the great German philosophers and of the dialectics sustained by them in a swamp of empty eclecticism, so much so that we are compelled to appeal to modern natural science as a witness for the affirmation of dialectics in actuality—we German socialists are proud of the fact that we are descendants not only of Saint-Simon, Fourier and Owen, but also of Kant, Fichte and Hegel.

Frederick Engels
September 1882

Introduction to the first English edition

THE PRESENT little book is, originally, a part of a larger whole. About 1875, Dr E Dühring, *privat-docent* at Berlin University, suddenly and rather clamorously announced his conversion to socialism, and presented the German public not only with an elaborate socialist theory, but also with a complete practical plan for the reorganisation of society. As a matter of course, he fell foul of his predecessors; above all, he honoured Marx by pouring out upon him the full vials of his wrath.

This took place about the time when the two sections of the Socialist Party in Germany—Eisenachers and Lassallians—had just effected their fusion, and thus obtained not only an immense increase of strength, but, what was more, the faculty of employing the whole of this strength against the common enemy. The Socialist Party in Germany was fast becoming a power. But to make it a power, the first condition was that the newly conquered unity should not be imperilled. And Dr Dühring openly proceeded to form around himself a sect, the nucleus of a future separate party. It thus became necessary to take up the gauntlet thrown down to us, and to fight out the struggle whether we liked it or not.

This, however, though it might not be an over-difficult, was evidently a long-winded business. As is well known, we Germans are of a terribly ponderous *Gründlichkeit*, radical profundity or profound radicality, whatever you may like to call it. Whenever any one of us expounds what he considers a new doctrine, he has first to elaborate it into an all-comprising system. He has to prove that both the first principles of logic and the fundamental laws of the universe had existed from all eternity for no other purpose than to ultimately lead to this newly discovered, crowning theory. And Dr Dühring, in this respect, was quite up to the national mark. Nothing less than a complete *System of Philosophy*, mental, moral, natural, and historical; a complete *System of Political Economy and Socialism*; and, finally, a *Critical History of Political Economy*—three big volumes in octavo, heavy extrinsically and intrinsically, three army corps of arguments mobilised against all previous philosophers and economists in general, and against Marx in particular— in fact, an attempt at a complete 'revolution in science'— these were what I should have to tackle.[1] I had to treat of all and every possible subject, from the concepts of time and space to bimetallism; from the eternity of matter and motion to the perishable nature of moral ideas; from Darwin's natural selection to the education of youth in a future society. Anyhow, the systematic comprehensiveness of my opponent gave me the opportunity of developing, in opposition to him, and in a more connected form than had previously been done, the views held by Marx and myself on this great variety of subjects. And that was the principal reason which made me undertake this otherwise ungrateful task.

My reply was first published in a series of articles in the Leipzig *Vorwärts*, the chief organ of the Socialist Party, and later on as a book: *Herr Eugen Dühring's Umwälzung der Wissenschaft* (*Mr E Dühring's Revolution in Science*), a second edition of which appeared in Zurich, 1886.

At the request of my friend, Paul Lafargue, now representative of Lille in the French Chamber of Deputies, I arranged three chapters of this book as a pamphlet, which he translated and published in 1880, under the title: *Socialisme utopique et socialisme scientifique*. From this French text a Polish and a Spanish edition were prepared. In 1883, our German friends brought out the pamphlet in the original language. Italian, Russian, Danish, Dutch, and Romanian translations, based upon the German text, have since been published. Thus, with the present English edition, this little book circulates in ten languages. I am not aware that any other socialist work, not even our *Communist Manifesto* of 1848 or Marx's *Capital*, has been so often translated. In Germany it has had four editions of about 20,000 copies in all.

The appendix, 'The Mark', was written with the intention of spreading among the German Socialist Party some elementary knowledge of the history and development of landed property in Germany.[2] This seemed all the more necessary at a time when the assimilation by that party of the working people of the towns was in a fair way of completion, and when the agricultural labourers and peasants had to be taken in hand. This appendix has been included in the translation, as the original forms of tenure of land common to all Teutonic tribes, and the history of their decay, are even less known in

27

England than in Germany. I have left the text as it stands in the original, without alluding to the hypothesis recently stated by Maxim Kovalevsky, according to which the partition of the arable and meadow lands among the members of the Mark was preceded by their being cultivated for joint account by a large patriarchal family community embracing several generations (as exemplified by the still existing South Slavonian Zadruga), and that the partition, later on, took place when the community had increased, so as to become too unwieldy for joint account management. Kovalevsky is probably quite right, but the matter is still *sub judice*.

The economic terms used in this work, as far as they are new, agree with those used in the English edition of Marx's *Capital*. We call 'production of commodities' that economic phase where articles are produced not only for the use of the producers, but also for purposes of exchange; that is, *as commodities*, not as use values. This phase extends from the first beginnings of production for exchange down to our present time; it attains its full development under capitalist production only, that is, under conditions where the capitalist, the owner of the means of production, employs, for wages, labourers, people deprived of all means of production except their own labour power, and pockets the excess of the selling price of the products over his outlay. We divide the history of industrial production since the Middle Ages into three periods: (1) handicraft, small master craftsmen with a few journeymen and apprentices, where each labourer produces the complete article; (2) manufacture, where greater numbers of workmen, grouped in one large establishment, produce the complete article on the principle of division of labour, each workman performing only one partial operation, so that the product is complete only after having passed successively through the hands of all; (3) modern industry, where the product is produced by machinery driven by power, and where the work of the labourer is limited to superintending and correcting the performances of the mechanical agent.

I am perfectly aware that the contents of this work will meet with objection from a considerable portion of the British public. But if we Continentals had taken the slightest notice of the prejudices of British 'respectability', we should be even worse off than we are. This book defends what we call 'historical materialism', and the word materialism grates upon the ears of the immense majority of British readers. 'Agnosticism' might be tolerated, but materialism is utterly inadmissible.

And yet the original home of all modern materialism, from the seventeenth century onwards, is England.

'Materialism is the natural-born son of Great Britain. Already the British schoolman, Duns Scotus, asked, "whether it was impossible for matter to think?"

'In order to effect this miracle, he took refuge in God's omnipotence, ie, he made theology preach materialism. Moreover, he was a nominalist.[3] Nominalism, the first form of materialism, is chiefly found among the English schoolmen.

'The real progenitor of English materialism is Bacon. To him natural philosophy is the only true philosophy, and physics based upon the experience of the senses is the chiefest part of natural philosophy. Anaxagoras and his homoiomeriae, Democritus and his atoms, he often quotes as his authorities.[4]

29

According to him the senses are infallible and the source of all knowledge. All science is based on experience, and consists in subjecting the data furnished by the senses to a rational method of investigation. Induction, analysis, comparison, observation, experiment, are the principal forms of such a rational method. Among the qualities inherent in matter, motion is the first and foremost, not only in the form of mechanical and mathematical motion, but chiefly in the form of an impulse, a vital spirit, a tension—or a "qual", to use a term of Jacob Böhme's—of matter.[5]

'In Bacon, its first creator, materialism still occludes within itself the germs of a many sided development. On the one hand, matter, surrounded by a sensuous, poetic glamour, seems to attract man's whole entity by winning smiles. On the other, the aphoristically formulated doctrine pullulates with inconsistencies imported from theology.

'In its further evolution, materialism becomes one sided. Hobbes is the man who systematises Baconian materialism. Knowledge based upon the senses loses its poetic blossom, it passes into the abstract experience of the mathematician; geometry is proclaimed as the queen of sciences. Materialism takes to misanthropy. If it is to overcome its opponent, misanthropic, fleshless spiritualism, and that on the latter's own ground, materialism has to chastise its own flesh and turn ascetic. Thus, from a sensual, it passes into an intellectual, entity; but thus, too, it evolves all the consistency, regardless of consequences, characteristic of the intellect.

'Hobbes, as Bacon's continuator, argues thus: if all human knowledge is furnished by the senses, then our concepts and ideas are but the phantoms, divested of their sensual forms, of the real world. Philosophy can but give names to these phantoms. One name may be applied to more than one of them. There may even be names of names. It would imply a contradiction if, on the one hand, we maintained that all ideas had their origin in the world of sensation, and, on the other, that a word was more than a word; that besides the beings known to us by our senses, beings which are one and all individuals, there existed also beings of a general, not individual, nature. An unbodily substance is the same absurdity as an unbodily body. Body, being, substance, are but different terms for the same reality. *It is impossible to separate thought from matter that thinks*. This matter is the substratum of all changes going on in the world. The word infinite is meaningless, unless it states that our mind is capable of performing an endless process of addition. Only material things being perceptible to us, we cannot know anything about the existence of God. My own existence alone is certain. Every human passion is a mechanical movement which has a beginning and an end. The objects of impulse are what we call good. Man is subject to the same laws as nature. Power and freedom are identical.

'Hobbes had systematised Bacon, without, however, furnishing a proof for Bacon's fundamental principle, the origin of all human knowledge from the world of sensation. It was Locke who, in his *Essay on the Human Understanding*, supplied this proof.

'Hobbes had shattered the theistic prejudices of Baconian materialism; Collins, Dodwell, Coward, Hartley, Priestley, similarly shattered the last theological bars that still hemmed in Locke's sensationalism. At all events, for practical materialists, deism is but an easy-going way of getting rid of religion.'[6]

Thus Karl Marx wrote about the British origin of modern materialism. If Englishmen nowadays do not exactly relish the compliment he paid their ancestors, more's the pity. It is none the less undeniable that Bacon, Hobbes, and Locke are the fathers of that brilliant school of French materialists which made the eighteenth century, in spite of all battles on land and sea won over Frenchmen by Germans and Englishmen, a pre-eminently French century, even before that crowning French Revolution, the results of which we outsiders, in England as well as in Germany, are still trying to acclimatise.

There is no denying it. About the middle of this century, what struck every cultivated foreigner who set up his residence in England, was what he was then bound to consider the religious bigotry and stupidity of the English respectable middle class. We, at that time, were all materialists, or, at least, very advanced freethinkers, and to us it appeared inconceivable that almost all educated people in England should believe in all sorts of impossible miracles, and that even geologists like Buckland and Mantell should contort the facts of their science so as not to clash too much with the myths of the book of Genesis; while, in order to find people who dared to use their own intellectual faculties with regard to religious matters, you had to go amongst the uneducated, the 'great unwashed', as they were then called, the working people, especially the Owenite socialists.

But England has been 'civilised' since then. The exhibition of 1851 sounded the knell of English insular exclusiveness. England became gradually

32

internationalised—in diet, in manners, in ideas; so much so that I begin to wish that some English manners and customs had made as much headway on the Continent as other Continental habits have made here. Anyhow, the introduction and spread of salad oil (before 1851 known only to the aristocracy) has been accompanied by a fatal spread of Continental scepticism in matters religious, and it has come to this, that agnosticism, though not yet considered 'the thing' quite as much as the Church of England, is yet very nearly on a par, as far as respectability goes, with Baptism, and decidedly ranks above the Salvation Army. And I cannot help believing that under these circumstances it will be consoling to many who sincerely regret and condemn this progress of infidelity to learn that these 'new-fangled notions' are not of foreign origin, are not 'made in Germany', like so many other articles of daily use, but are undoubtedly Old English, and that their British originators 200 years ago went a good deal further than their descendants now dare to venture.

What, indeed, is agnosticism, but, to use an expressive Lancashire term, 'shamefaced' materialism? The agnostic's conception of Nature is materialistic throughout. The entire natural world is governed by law, and absolutely excludes the intervention of action from without. But, he adds, we have no means either of ascertaining or of disproving the existence of some Supreme Being beyond the known universe. Now, this might hold good at the time when Laplace, to Napoleon's question, why in the great astronomer's *Mécanique céleste* [Celestial mechanics] the Creator was not even mentioned, proudly replied: *Je n'avais pas besoin de cette hypothèse* [I had no need for this hypothesis]. But

33

nowadays, in our evolutionary conception of the universe, there is absolutely no room for either a Creator or a Ruler; and to talk of a Supreme Being shut out from the whole existing world, implies a contradiction in terms, and, as it seems to me, a gratuitous insult to the feelings of religious people.

Again, our agnostic admits that all our knowledge is based upon the information imparted to us by our senses. But, he adds, how do we know that our senses give us correct representations of the objects we perceive through them? And he proceeds to inform us that, whenever he speaks of objects or their qualities, he does in reality not mean these objects and qualities, of which he cannot know anything for certain, but merely the impressions which they have produced on his senses. Now, this line of reasoning seems undoubtedly hard to beat by mere argumentation. But before there was argumentation, there was action. *Im Anfang war die Tat* [In the beginning was the deed]. And human action had solved the difficulty long before human ingenuity invented it. The proof of the pudding is in the eating. From the moment we turn to our own use these objects, according to the qualities we perceive in them, we put to an infallible test the correctness or otherwise of our sense perceptions. If these perceptions have been wrong, then our estimate of the use to which an object can be turned must also be wrong, and our attempt must fail. But if we succeed in accomplishing our aim, if we find that the object does agree with our idea of it, and does answer the purpose we intended it for, then that is positive proof that our perceptions of it and of its qualities, so far, agree with reality outside ourselves. And whenever we find ourselves face to face with a failure, then we generally are not long in making out the cause that made us fail; we find that the perception upon which we acted was either incomplete and superficial, or combined with the results of other perceptions in a way not warranted by them—what we call defective reasoning. So long as we take care to train and to use our senses properly, and to keep our action within the limits prescribed by perceptions properly made and properly used, so long we shall find that the result of our action proves the conformity of our perceptions with the objective nature of the things perceived. Not in one single instance, so far, have we been led to the conclusion that our sense perceptions, scientifically controlled, induce in our minds ideas respecting the outer world that are, by their very nature, at variance with reality, or that there is an inherent incompatibility between the outer world and our sense perceptions of it.

But then come the Neo-Kantian agnostics and say: We may correctly perceive the qualities of a thing, but we cannot by any sensible or mental process grasp the thing-in-itself. This 'thing-in-itself' is beyond our ken. To this Hegel, long since, has replied: If you know all the qualities of a thing, you know the thing itself; nothing remains but the fact that the said thing exists without us; and when your senses have taught you that fact, you have grasped the last remnant of the thing-in-itself, Kant's celebrated unknowable *Ding an sich*. To which it may be added, that in Kant's time our knowledge of natural objects was indeed so fragmentary that he might well suspect, behind the little we knew about each of them, a mysterious 'thing-in-itself'. But one after another these ungraspable things have been grasped, analysed, and, what is more, *reproduced* by the giant progress of science; and what we can produce, we certainly cannot consider as unknowable. To the chemistry of the first half of this century organic substances were such mysterious objects; now we learn to build them up one after another from their chemical elements without the aid of organic processes. Modern chemists declare that as soon as the chemical constitution of no matter what body is known, it can be built up from its elements. We are still far from knowing the constitution of the highest organic substances, the albuminous bodies [proteins]; but there is no reason why we should not, if only after centuries, arrive at that knowledge and, armed with it, produce artificial albumen. But if we arrive at that, we shall at the same time have produced organic life, for life, from its lowest to its highest forms, is but the normal mode of existence of albuminous bodies.

As soon, however, as our agnostic has made these formal mental reservations, he talks and acts as the rank materialist he at bottom is. He may say that, as far as *we* know, matter and motion, or as it is now called, energy, can neither be created nor destroyed, but that we have no proof of their not having been created at some time or other. But if you try to use this admission against him in any particular case, he will quickly put you out of court. If he admits the possibility of spiritualism *in abstracto* [in the abstract], he will have none of it *in concreto* [concretely]. As far as we know and can know, he will tell you there is no Creator and no Ruler of the universe; as far as we are concerned, matter and energy can neither be created nor annihilated; for us, mind is a mode of energy, a function of the brain; all we know is that the material world is governed by immutable laws, and so forth. Thus, as far as he is a scientific man, as far as he *knows* anything, he is a materialist; outside his science, in spheres about which he knows nothing, he translates his ignorance into Greek and calls it agnosticism.

At all events, one thing seems clear: even if I was an agnostic, it is evident that I could not describe the conception of history sketched out in this little book as 'historical agnosticism'. Religious people would laugh at me, agnostics would indignantly ask: Was I going to make fun of them? And thus I hope even British respectability will not be overshocked if I use, in English as well as in so many other languages, the term, 'historical materialism', to designate that view of the course of history which seeks the ultimate cause and the great moving power of all important historic events in the economic development of society, in the changes in the modes of production and exchange, in the consequent division of society into distinct classes, and in the struggles of these classes against one another.

This indulgence will perhaps be accorded to me all the sooner if I show that historical materialism may be of advantage even to British respectability. I have mentioned the fact, that about 40 or 50 years ago, any cultivated foreigner settling in England was struck by what he was then bound to consider the religious bigotry and stupidity of the English respectable middle class. I am now going to prove that the respectable English middle class of that time was not quite as stupid as it looked to the intelligent foreigner. Its religious leanings can be explained.

When Europe emerged from the Middle Ages, the rising middle class of the towns constituted its revolutionary element. It had conquered a recognised position within mediaeval feudal organisation, but this position, also, had become too narrow for its expansive power. The development of the middle class, the *bourgeoisie*, became incompatible with the maintenance of the feudal system; the feudal system, therefore, had to fall.

But the great international centre of feudalism was the Roman Catholic Church. It united the whole of feudalised Western Europe, in spite of all internal wars, into one grand political system, opposed as much to the schismatic Greeks as to the Mohammedan countries. It surrounded feudal institutions with the halo of divine consecration. It had organised its own hierarchy on the feudal model, and, lastly, it was itself by far the most powerful feudal lord, holding, as it did, fully one third of the soil of the Catholic world. Before profane feudalism could be successfully attacked in each country and in detail, this, its sacred central organisation, had to be destroyed.

Moreover, parallel with the rise of the middle class went on the great revival of science; astronomy, mechanics, physics, anatomy, physiology, were again cultivated. And the bourgeoisie, for the development of its industrial production, required a science which ascertained the physical properties of natural objects and the modes of action of the forces of Nature. Now up to then science had but been the humble handmaid of the Church, had not been allowed to overstep the limits set by faith, and for that reason had been no science at all. Science rebelled against the Church; the bourgeoisie could not do without science, and, therefore, had to join in the rebellion.

The above, though touching but two of the points where the rising middle class was bound to come into collision with the established religion, will be sufficient to show, first, that the class most directly interested in the struggle against the pretensions of the Roman Church was the bourgeoisie; and second, that every struggle against feudalism, at that time, had to take on a religious disguise, had to be directed against the Church in the first instance. But if the universities and the traders of the cities started the cry, it was sure to find, and did find, a strong echo in the masses of the country people, the peasants, who everywhere had to struggle for their very existence with their feudal lords, spiritual and temporal.

The long fight of the bourgeoisie against feudalism culminated in three great, decisive battles.

The first was what is called the Protestant Reformation in Germany. The war cry raised against the Church by Luther was responded to by two insurrections of a political nature: first, that of the lower nobility under Franz von Sickingen (1523), then the great Peasants' War, 1525. Both were defeated, chiefly in consequence of the indecision of the parties most interested, the burghers of the towns—an indecision into the causes of which we cannot here enter. From that moment the struggle degenerated into a fight between the local princes and the central power, and ended by blotting out Germany, for two hundred years, from the politically active nations of Europe. The Lutheran Reformation produced a new creed indeed, a religion adapted to absolute monarchy. No sooner were the peasants of north east Germany converted to Lutheranism than they were from freemen reduced to serfs.

But where Luther failed, Calvin won the day. Calvin's creed was one fit for the boldest of the bourgeoisie of his time. His predestination doctrine was the religious expression of the fact that in the commercial world of competition success or failure does not depend upon a man's activity or cleverness, but upon circumstances uncontrollable by him. It is not of him that willeth or of him that runneth, but of the mercy of unknown superior economic powers; and this was especially true at a period of economic revolution, when all old commercial routes and centres were replaced by new ones, when India and America were opened to the world, and when even the most sacred economic articles of faith— the value of gold and silver—began to totter and to break down. Calvin's church constitution was thoroughly democratic and republican; and where the kingdom of God was republicanised, could the kingdoms of this world remain subject to monarchs, bishops, and lords? While German Lutheranism became a willing tool in the hands of princes, Calvinism founded a republic in Holland, and active republican parties in England, and, above all, Scotland.

In Calvinism, the second great bourgeois upheaval found its doctrine ready cut and dried. This upheaval took place in England. The middle class of the towns brought it on, and the yeomanry of the country districts fought it out. Curiously enough, in all the three great bourgeois risings, the peasantry furnishes the army that has to do the fighting; and the peasantry is just the class that, the victory once gained, is most surely ruined by the economic consequences of that victory. A hundred years after Cromwell, the yeomanry of England had almost disappeared. Anyhow, had it not been for that yeomanry and for the *plebeian* element in the towns, the bourgeoisie alone would never have fought the matter out to the bitter end, and would never have brought Charles I to the scaffold. In order to secure even those conquests of the bourgeoisie that were ripe for gathering at the time, the revolution had to be carried considerably further—exactly as in 1793 in France and 1848 in Germany. This seems, in fact, to be one of the laws of evolution of bourgeois society.

Well, upon this excess of revolutionary activity there necessarily followed the inevitable reaction which in its turn went beyond the point where it might have maintained itself. After a series of oscillations, the new centre of gravity was at last attained and became a new starting point. The grand period of English history, known to respectability under the name of 'the Great Rebellion', and the struggles succeeding it, were brought to a close by the comparatively puny event entitled by Liberal historians, 'the Glorious Revolution'.

The new starting point was a compromise between the rising middle class and the ex-feudal landowners. The latter, though called, as now, the aristocracy, had been long since on the way which led them to become what Louis Philippe in France became at a much later period, 'the first bourgeois of the kingdom'. Fortunately for England, the old feudal barons had killed one another during the Wars of the Roses. Their successors, though mostly scions of the old families, had been so much out of the direct line of descent that they constituted quite a new body, with habits and tendencies far more bourgeois than feudal. They fully understood the value of money, and at once began to increase their rents by turning hundreds of small farmers out and replacing them by sheep. Henry VIII, while squandering the Church lands, created fresh bourgeois landlords by wholesale; the innumerable confiscations of estates, regranted to absolute or relative upstarts, and continued during the whole of the seventeenth century, had the same result. Consequently, ever since Henry VII, the English 'aristocracy', far from counteracting the development of industrial production, had, on the contrary, sought to indirectly profit thereby; and there had always been a section of the great landowners willing, from economical or political reasons, to co-operate with the leading men of the financial and industrial bourgeoisie. The compromise of 1689 was, therefore, easily accomplished. The political spoils of 'pelf and place' were left to the great landowning families, provided the economic interests of the financial, manufacturing, and commercial middle class were sufficiently attended to. And these economic interests were at that time powerful enough to determine the general policy of the nation. There might be squabbles about matters of detail, but, on the whole, the aristocratic oligarchy knew too well that its own economic prosperity was irretrievably bound up with that of the industrial and commercial middle class.

From that time, the bourgeoisie was a humble, but still a recognised component of the ruling classes of England. With the rest of them, it had a common interest in keeping in subjection the great working mass of the nation. The merchant or manufacturer himself stood in the position of master, or, as it was until lately called, of 'natural superior' to his clerks, his workpeople, his domestic servants. His interest was to get as much and as good work out of them as he could; for this end they had to be trained to proper submission. He was himself religious; his religion had supplied the standard under which he had fought the king and the lords; he was not long in discovering the opportunities this same religion offered him for working upon the minds of his natural inferiors, and making them submissive to the behests of the masters it had pleased God to place over them. In short, the English bourgeoisie now had to take a part in keeping down the 'lower orders', the great producing mass of the nation, and one of the means employed for that purpose was the influence of religion.

There was another fact that contributed to strengthen the religious leanings of the bourgeoisie. That was the rise of materialism in England. This new doctrine not only shocked the pious feelings of the middle class; it announced itself as a philosophy only fit for scholars and cultivated men of the world, in contrast to religion which was good enough for the uneducated masses, including the bourgeoisie. With Hobbes it stepped on the stage as a defender of royal prerogative and omnipotence; it called upon absolute monarchy to keep down that *puer robustus sed malitiosus* [robust but malicious boy], to wit, the people. Similarly, with the successors of Hobbes, with Bolingbroke, Shaftesbury, etc, the new deistic form of materialism remained an aristocratic, esoteric doctrine, and, therefore, hateful to the middle class both for its religious heresy and for its anti bourgeois political connections. Accordingly, in opposition to the materialism and deism of the aristocracy, those Protestant sects which had furnished the flag and the fighting contingent against the Stuarts, continued to furnish the main strength of the progressive middle class, and form even today the backbone of 'the Great Liberal Party'.

In the meantime materialism passed from England to France, where it met and coalesced with another materialistic school of philosophers, a branch of Cartesianism. In France, too, it remained at first an exclusively aristocratic doctrine. But soon its revolutionary character asserted itself. The French materialists did not limit their criticism to matters of religious belief; they extended it to whatever scientific tradition or political institution they met with; and to prove the claim of their doctrine to universal application, they took the shortest cut, and boldly applied it to all subjects of knowledge in the giant work after which they were named—the *Encyclopédie*. Thus, in one or the other of its two forms—avowed materialism or deism—it became the creed of the whole cultured youth of France; so much so that, when the Great Revolution broke out, the doctrine hatched by English Royalists gave a theoretical flag to French Republicans and Terrorists, and furnished the text for the Declaration of the Rights of Man. The Great French Revolution was the third uprising of the bourgeoisie, but the first that had entirely cast off the religious cloak, and was fought out on undisguised political lines; it was the first, too, that was really fought out up to the destruction of one of the combatants, the aristocracy, and the complete triumph of the other, the bourgeoisie. In England the continuity of pre-revolutionary and post-revolutionary institutions, and the compromise between landlords and capitalists, found its expression in the continuity of judicial precedents and in the religious preservation of the feudal forms of the law. In France the Revolution constituted a complete breach with the traditions of the past; it cleared out the very last vestiges of feudalism, and created in

44

the *Code civil* a masterly adaptation of the old Roman law—that almost perfect expression of the juridical relations corresponding to the economic stage called by Marx the production of commodities—to modern capitalistic conditions; so masterly that this French revolutionary code still serves as a model for reforms of the law of property in all other countries, not excepting England. Let us, however, not forget that if English law continues to express the economic relations of capitalistic society in that barbarous feudal language which corresponds to the thing expressed, just as English spelling corresponds to English pronunciation—*vous écrivez Londres et vous prononcez Constantinople* [You write London and pronounce it Constantinople], said a Frenchman—that same English law is the only one which has preserved through ages, and transmitted to America and the Colonies, the best part of that old Germanic personal freedom, local self government, and independence from all interference but that of the law courts which on the Continent has been lost during the period of absolute monarchy, and has nowhere been as yet fully recovered.

To return to our British bourgeois. The French Revolution gave him a splendid opportunity, with the help of the Continental monarchies, to destroy French maritime commerce, to annex French colonies, and to crush the last French pretensions to maritime rivalry. That was one reason why he fought it. Another was that the ways of this revolution went very much against his grain. Not only its 'execrable' terrorism, but the very attempt to carry bourgeois rule to extremes. What should the British bourgeois do without his aristocracy, that taught him manners, such as they were, and invented fashions for him—

that furnished officers for the army, which kept order at home, and the navy, which conquered colonial possessions and new markets abroad? There was indeed a progressive minority of the bourgeoisie, that minority whose interests were not so well attended to under the compromise; this section, composed chiefly of the less wealthy middle class, did sympathise with the Revolution, but it was powerless in Parliament.

Thus, if materialism became the creed of the French Revolution, the God fearing English bourgeois held all the faster to his religion. Had not the reign of terror in Paris proved what was the upshot, if the religious instincts of the masses were lost? The more materialism spread from France to neighbouring countries, and was reinforced by similar doctrinal currents, notably by German philosophy, the more, in fact, materialism and freethought generally became on the Continent the necessary qualifications of a cultivated man, the more stubbornly the English middle class stuck to its manifold religious creeds. These creeds might differ from one another, but they were, all of them, distinctly religious, Christian creeds.

While the Revolution ensured the political triumph of the bourgeoisie in France, in England Watt, Arkwright, Cartwright, and others, initiated an industrial revolution, which completely shifted the centre of gravity of economic power. The wealth of the bourgeoisie increased considerably faster than that of the landed aristocracy. Within the bourgeoisie itself the financial aristocracy, the bankers, etc, were more and more pushed into the background by the manufacturers. The compromise of 1689, even after the gradual changes it had undergone in favour of the bourgeoisie, no longer corresponded to the relative position of the parties to it. The character of these parties, too, had changed; the bourgeoisie of 1830 was very different from that of the preceding century. The political power still left to the aristocracy, and used by them to resist the pretensions of the new industrial bourgeoisie, became incompatible with the new economic interests. A fresh struggle with the aristocracy was necessary; it could end only in a victory of the new economic power. First, the Reform Act was pushed through, in spite of all resistance, under the impulse of the French Revolution of 1830. It gave to the bourgeoisie a recognised and powerful place in Parliament. Then the repeal of the Corn Laws, which settled, once for all, the supremacy of the bourgeoisie, and especially of its most active portion, the manufacturers, over the landed aristocracy. This was the greatest victory of the bourgeoisie; it was, however, also the last it gained in its own exclusive interest. Whatever triumphs it obtained later on, it had to share with a new social power, first its ally, but soon its rival.

The industrial revolution had created a class of large manufacturing capitalists, but also a class— and a far more numerous one—of manufacturing workpeople. This class gradually increased in numbers, in proportion as the industrial revolution seized upon one branch of manufacture after another, and in the same proportion it increased in power. This power it proved as early as 1824, by forcing a reluctant Parliament to repeal the acts forbidding combinations of workmen. During the Reform agitation, the working men constituted the Radical wing of the Reform Party; the Act of 1832 having excluded them from the suffrage, they formulated their demands in the People's Charter, and constituted themselves, in opposition to the great bourgeois Anti Corn Law party, into an independent party, the Chartists, the first working men's party of modern times.

Then came the Continental revolutions of February and March, 1848, in which the working people played such a prominent part, and, at least in Paris, put forward demands which were certainly inadmissible from the point of view of capitalist society. And then came the general reaction. First the defeat of the Chartists on 10 April 1848, then the crushing of the Paris working men's insurrection in June of the same year, then the disasters of 1849 in Italy, Hungary, south Germany, and at last the victory of Louis Bonaparte over Paris, 2 December 1851. For a time, at least, the bugbear of working class pretensions was put down, but at what cost! If the British bourgeois had been convinced before of the necessity of maintaining the common people in a religious mood, how much more must he feel that necessity after all these experiences? Regardless of the sneers of his Continental compeers, he continued to spend thousands and tens of thousands, year after year, upon the evangelisation of the lower orders; not content with his own native religious machinery, he appealed to Brother Jonathan, the greatest organiser in existence of religion as a trade, and imported from America revivalism, Moody and Sankey, and the like; and, finally, he accepted the dangerous aid of the Salvation Army, which revives the propaganda of early Christianity, appeals to the poor as the elect, fights capitalism in a religious way, and thus fosters an element of early Christian class antagonism, which one day may become troublesome to the well to do people who now find the ready money for it.

It seems a law of historical development that the bourgeoisie can in no European country get hold of political power—at least for any length of time—in the same exclusive way in which the feudal aristocracy kept hold of it during the Middle Ages. Even in France, where feudalism was completely extinguished, the bourgeoisie, as a whole, has held full possession of the Government for very short periods only. During Louis Philippe's reign, 1830-48, a very small portion of the bourgeoisie ruled the kingdom; by far the larger part were excluded from the suffrage by the high qualification. Under the Second Republic, 1848-51, the whole bourgeoisie ruled, but for three years only; their incapacity brought on the Second Empire. It is only now, in the Third Republic, that the bourgeoisie as a whole have kept possession of the helm for more than 20 years; and they are already showing lively signs of decadence. A durable reign of the bourgeoisie has been possible only in countries like America, where feudalism was unknown, and society at the very beginning started from a bourgeois basis. And even in France and America, the successors of the bourgeoisie, the working people, are already knocking at the door.

In England, the bourgeoisie never held undivided sway. Even the victory of 1832 left the landed aristocracy in almost exclusive possession of all the leading Government offices. The meekness with which the wealthy middle class submitted to this remained inconceivable to me until the great Liberal manufacturer, Mr WA Forster, in a public speech implored the young men of Bradford to learn French, as a means to get on in the world, and quoted from his own experience how sheepish he looked when, as a cabinet minister, he had to move in society where

49

French was, at least, as necessary as English! The fact was, the English middle class of that time were, as a rule, quite uneducated upstarts, and could not help leaving to the aristocracy those superior Government places where other qualifications were required than mere insular narrowness and insular conceit, seasoned by business sharpness.[7] Even now the endless newspaper debates about middle class education show that the English middle class does not yet consider itself good enough for the best education, and looks to something more modest. Thus, even after the repeal of the Corn Laws, it appeared a matter of course that the men who had carried the day, the Cobdens, Brights, Forsters, etc, should remain excluded from a share in the official government of the country, until 20 years afterwards, a new Reform Act opened to them the door of the cabinet. The English bourgeoisie are, up to the present day, so deeply penetrated by a sense of their social inferiority that they keep up, at their own expense and that of the nation, an ornamental caste of drones to represent the nation worthily at all state functions; and they consider themselves highly honoured whenever one of themselves is found worthy of admission into this select and privileged body, manufactured, after all, by themselves.

The industrial and commercial middle class had, therefore, not yet succeeded in driving the landed aristocracy completely from political power when another competitor, the working class, appeared on the stage. The reaction after the Chartist movement and the Continental revolutions, as well as the unparalleled extension of English trade from 1848-66 (ascribed vulgarly to Free Trade alone, but due far more to the colossal development of railways, ocean steamers, and means of intercourse generally), had again driven the working class into the dependency of the Liberal Party, of which they formed, as in pre-Chartist times, the Radical wing. Their claims to the franchise, however, gradually became irresistible; while the Whig leaders of the Liberals 'funked', Disraeli showed his superiority by making the Tories seize the favourable moment and introduce household suffrage in the boroughs, along with a redistribution of seats. Then followed the ballot; then in 1884 the extension of household suffrage to the counties and a fresh redistribution of seats, by which electoral districts were to some extent equalised. All these measures considerably increased the electoral power of the working class, so much so that in at least 150 to 200 constituencies that class now furnishes the majority of voters. But parliamentary government is a capital school for teaching respect for tradition; if the middle class look with awe and veneration upon what Lord John Manners playfully called 'our old nobility', the mass of the working people then looked up with respect and deference to what used to be designated as 'their betters', the middle class. Indeed, the British workman, some 15 years ago, was the model workman, whose respectful regard for the position of his master, and whose self restraining modesty in claiming rights for himself, consoled our German economists of the Katheder Socialist school for the incurable communistic and revolutionary tendencies of their own working men at home.[8]

But the English middle class—good men of business as they are—saw farther than the German professors. They had shared their power but reluctantly with the working class. They had learned, during the Chartist years, what that *puer robustus sed malitiosus*, the people, is capable of. And since that time, they had been compelled to incorporate the better part of the People's Charter in the Statutes of the United Kingdom. Now, if ever, the people must be kept in order by moral means, and the first and foremost of all moral means of action upon the masses is and remains—religion. Hence the parsons' majorities on the school boards, hence the increasing self taxation of the bourgeoisie for the support of all sorts of revivalism, from ritualism to the Salvation Army.

And now came the triumph of British respectability over the freethought and religious laxity of the Continental bourgeois. The workmen of France and Germany had become rebellious. They were thoroughly infected with socialism, and, for very good reasons, were not at all particular as to the legality of the means by which to secure their own ascendency. The *puer robustus*, here, turned from day to day more *malitiosus*. Nothing remained to the French and German bourgeoisie as a last resource but to silently drop their freethought, as a youngster, when sea sickness creeps upon him, quietly drops the burning cigar he brought swaggeringly on board; one by one, the scoffers turned pious in outward behaviour, spoke with respect of the Church, its dogmas and rites, and even conformed with the latter as far as could not be helped. French bourgeois dined *maigre* [meagrely] on Fridays, and German ones sat out long Protestant sermons in their pews on Sundays. They had come to grief with materialism. '*Die Religion muss dem Volk erhalten werden*'—religion must be kept alive for the people—that was the only and the last means to save society from utter ruin.

Unfortunately for themselves, they did not find this out until they had done their level best to break up religion for ever. And now it was the turn of the British bourgeois to sneer and to say: 'Why, you fools, I could have told you that 200 years ago!'

However, I am afraid neither the religious stolidity of the British, nor the *post festum* [after the event] conversion of the Continental bourgeois will stem the rising proletarian tide. Tradition is a great retarding force, is the *vis inertiae* [inertia] of history, but, being merely passive, is sure to be broken down; and thus religion will be no lasting safeguard to capitalist society. If our juridical, philosophical, and religious ideas are the more or less remote offshoots of the economical relations prevailing in a given society, such ideas cannot, in the long run, withstand the effects of a complete change in these relations. And, unless we believe in supernatural revelation, we must admit that no religious tenets will ever suffice to prop up a tottering society.

In fact, in England too, the working people have begun to move again. They are, no doubt, shackled by traditions of various kinds. Bourgeois traditions, such as the widespread belief that there can be but two parties, Conservatives and Liberals, and that the working class must work out its salvation by and through the great Liberal Party. Working men's traditions, inherited from their first tentative efforts at independent action, such as the exclusion, from ever so many old Trade Unions, of all applicants who have not gone through a regular apprenticeship; which means the breeding, by every such union, of its own blacklegs. But for all that the English working class is moving, as even Professor Brentano has sorrowfully had to report to his brother Katheder

Socialists. It moves, like all things in England, with a slow and measured step, with hesitation here, with more or less unfruitful, tentative attempts there; it moves now and then with an over-cautious mistrust of the name of socialism, while it gradually absorbs the substance; and the movement spreads and seizes one layer of the workers after another. It has now shaken out of their torpor the unskilled labourers of the East End of London, and we all know what a splendid impulse these fresh forces have given it in return. And if the pace of the movement is not up to the impatience of some people, let them not forget that it is the working class which keeps alive the finest qualities of the English character, and that, if a step in advance is once gained in England, it is, as a rule, never lost afterwards. If the sons of the old Chartists, for reasons explained above, were not quite up to the mark, the grandsons bid fair to be worthy of their forefathers.

But the triumph of the European working class does not depend upon England alone. It can only be secured by the co-operation of, at least, England, France, and Germany. In both the latter countries the working class movement is well ahead of England. In Germany it is even within measurable distance of success. The progress it has there made during the last 25 years is unparalleled. It advances with ever-increasing velocity. If the German middle class have shown themselves lamentably deficient in political capacity, discipline, courage, energy, and perseverance, the German working class have given ample proof of all these qualities. 400 years ago, Germany was the starting point of the first upheaval of the European middle class; as things are now, is it outside the limits of possibility that Germany will be the scene, too, of the first great victory of the European proletariat?

Frederick Engels
April 1892

Chapter 1

MODERN SOCIALISM is, in its content, primarily the product of the recognition, on the one hand, of the class antagonisms prevailing in modern society between proprietors and non-proprietors, between capitalists and wage workers, and on the other, of the anarchy ruling in production. In its theoretical form, however, it originally appears as a more developed and allegedly more consistent extension of the principles laid down by the great French philosophers of the Enlightenment in the eighteenth century. Like every new theory, modern socialism had at first to link itself with the intellectual data ready to hand, however deeply its roots lay in material economic facts.

The great men who in France were clearing men's minds for the coming revolution acted in an extremely revolutionary way themselves. They recognised no external authority of any kind. Religion, conceptions of nature, society, political systems—everything was subjected to the most unsparing criticism: everything had to justify its existence before the judgment-seat of reason or give up existence. The reasoning intellect became the sole measure of everything. It was the time when, as

Hegel says, the world was stood on its head, first in the sense that the human head and the principles arrived at by its thinking claimed to be the basis of all human action and association; but then later also in the wider sense that the reality which was in contradiction with these principles was, in fact, turned upside down.[1] Every previous form of society and state, every old traditional notion was flung into the lumber-room as irrational; the world had hitherto allowed itself to be led solely by prejudice; everything in the past deserved only pity and contempt. The light of day, the realm of reason, now appeared for the first time; henceforth superstition, injustice, privilege and oppression were to be superseded by eternal truth, eternal justice, equality based on nature, and the inalienable rights of man.

We know today that this realm of reason was nothing more than the idealised realm of the bourgeoisie; that eternal justice found its realisation in bourgeois justice; that equality reduced itself to bourgeois equality before the law; that bourgeois property was proclaimed as one of the most essential rights of man; and that the government of reason, Rousseau's social contract, came into being, and could only come into being, as a bourgeois democratic republic. The great thinkers of the eighteenth century were no more able than their predecessors to go beyond the limits imposed on them by their own epoch.

But side by side with the antagonism of the feudal nobility and the burghers who claimed to represent all the rest of society, there was the general antagonism of exploiters and exploited, of the rich idlers and the toiling poor. It was precisely this circumstance that enabled the representatives of the bourgeoisie to put themselves forward as the representatives not of one special class but of the whole of suffering humanity. Still more. From its origin the bourgeoisie was saddled with its antithesis: capitalists cannot exist without wage workers, and, in the same proportion as the mediaeval burgher of the guild developed into the modern bourgeois, so the guild journeyman and the day labourer outside the guilds developed into the proletarian. And although, on the whole, the burghers *in their struggle with the nobility* could claim to represent at the same time the interests of the different working classes of that period, in every great bourgeois movement there were independent outbursts of that class which was the more or less developed forerunner of the modern proletariat. For example, at the time of the German Reformation and the Peasants' War, the Anabaptists and Thomas Münzer; in the great English Revolution, the Levellers; in the great French Revolution, Babeuf.[2]

There were theoretical manifestations corresponding with these revolutionary uprisings of an as yet immature class; in the sixteenth and seventeenth centuries, utopian pictures of ideal social conditions, in the eighteenth, direct communistic theories (Morelly and Mably). The demand for equality was no longer limited to political rights but was also extended to the social conditions of individuals; it was not merely class privileges that were to be abolished, but class distinctions themselves. An ascetic communism prohibiting all the pleasures of life copied from Sparta was thus the first form of the new teaching. Then came the three great Utopians: Saint-Simon, to whom the bourgeois current still had a certain significance side by side with the proletarian, Fourier, and Owen, who in the country where capitalist production was the most developed and under the influence of the antagonisms begotten by it systematically worked out his proposals for the abolition of class distinctions in direct relation to French materialism.

One thing is common to all three. Not one of them appears as a representative of the interests of the proletariat which historical development had in the meantime produced. Like the philosophers of the Enlightenment, they want to emancipate not a particular class to begin with, but all humanity at once. Like them, they wish to bring in the realm of reason and of eternal justice, but this realm is as far as heaven from earth from that of the philosophers of the Enlightenment. For the bourgeois world based upon the principles of these philosophers is also irrational and unjust and, therefore, finds its way to the dustbin just as readily as feudalism and all earlier orders of society. If pure reason and justice have not hitherto ruled the world, it is only because they have not been rightly understood. What was wanting was only the individual man of genius, who has now arisen and who has recognised the truth. The fact that he has now arisen, that the truth has been recognised precisely at this moment, is not an inevitable event following of necessity in the chain of historical development, but a mere happy accident. He might just as well have been born 500 years earlier and might then have spared humanity 500 years of error, strife and suffering.

We saw how the French philosophers of the eighteenth century, the forerunners of the Revolution, appealed to reason as the sole judge of everything in existence. A rational state, a rational society, were to be founded; everything running counter to eternal reason was to be remorselessly done away with. We saw also that this eternal reason was in reality nothing but the idealised understanding of the middle burgher, who was just then evolving into the bourgeois. But when the French Revolution had realised this rational society and state, the new order of things, however rational as compared with earlier conditions, proved to be by no means absolutely rational. The state based upon reason completely collapsed. Rousseau's social contract had found its realisation in the Reign of Terror, from which the bourgeoisie, after losing faith in its own political capacity, had taken refuge first in the corruption of the Directorate and finally under the wing of the Napoleonic despotism. The promised eternal peace was turned into an endless war of conquest. The society based upon reason had fared no better. Instead of dissolving into general prosperity, the antagonism between rich and poor had become sharpened by the elimination of the guild and other privileges, which had bridged it over, and of the charitable institutions of the Church, which had mitigated it. As far as the small capitalists and small peasants were concerned, the 'freedom of property' from feudal fetters, which had now become a reality, proved to be the freedom to sell their small property, which was being crushed under the overpowering competition of big capital and big landed property, to these very lords, so that freedom of property turned into 'freedom *from* property' for the small capitalists and peasant proprietors. The rapid growth of industry on a capitalist basis raised the poverty and misery of the working masses to a condition of existence of society. Cash payment increasingly became, in Carlyle's phrase, the sole social nexus. The number of crimes increased from year to year. Though not eradicated, the feudal vices which had previously been flaunted in broad daylight were now at any rate thrust into the background. In their stead, the bourgeois vices, hitherto nursed in secret, began to blossom all the more luxuriantly. Trade developed more and more into swindling. The 'fraternity' of the revolutionary slogan was realised in the chicanery and envy of the battle of competition. Oppression by force was replaced by corruption, the sword as the prime social lever by money. 'The right of the first night' passed from the feudal lords to the bourgeois manufacturers. Prostitution assumed hitherto unheard of proportions. Marriage itself remained as before the legally recognised form, the official cloak of prostitution, and, moreover, was copiously supplemented by adultery.

In short, the social and political institutions born of the 'triumph of reason' were bitterly disappointing caricatures of the splendid promises of the philosophers of the Enlightenment. All that was wanting was the men to formulate this disappointment, and they came with the turn of the century. Saint-Simon's *Letters from Geneva* appeared in 1802, Fourier's first book appeared in 1808, although the groundwork of his theory dated from 1799; Robert Owen took over the direction of New Lanark on 1 January 1800.[3]

At this time, however, the capitalist mode of production, and with it the antagonism between the bourgeoisie and the proletariat, was still very undeveloped. Large scale industry, which had only just arisen in England, was still unknown in France. But, on the one hand, large scale industry promotes the conflicts which make a revolution in the mode of production and the abolition of its capitalist character absolutely necessary—conflicts not only between the classes begotten of it, but also between precisely the productive forces and the forms of exchange created by it. On the other hand, it is in these gigantic productive forces themselves that it promotes the means of resolving these conflicts. If, therefore, the conflicts arising from the new social order were only just beginning to take shape around 1800, this is even truer for the means of resolving them. During the Reign of Terror, the propertyless masses of Paris were able to gain the mastery for a moment, and thus to lead the bourgeois revolution to victory *against* the bourgeoisie itself. But in doing so they only proved how impossible it was for their domination to last under the conditions then obtaining. The proletariat, which was only just separating itself from these propertyless masses as the nucleus of a new class and was as yet quite incapable of independent political action, appeared as an oppressed, suffering estate, to which, in its incapacity to help itself, help could at best be brought in from without, from above down.

This historical situation also dominated the founders of socialism. Their immature theories corresponded to the immature state of capitalist production and the immature class situation. The solution of the social problems which as yet lay hidden in undeveloped economic relations was to spring from the human brain. Society presented nothing but abuses; to remove them was the task of reflective reason. It was a question of inventing a new and more perfect social order and of imposing it on society from without, by propaganda and wherever possible by the example of model experiments. These new social systems were foredoomed to be Utopias; the more they were worked out in detail, the more inevitably they became lost in pure fantasy.

Having established this, we shall not dwell a moment longer on this aspect, now belonging wholly to the past. We can leave it to the literary small fry to quibble solemnly over these fantasies, which today only make us smile, and to crow over the superiority of their own sober reasoning over such 'insanity'. For ourselves, we delight in the inspired thoughts and germs of thought that everywhere break out through their fantastic covering and to which these philistines are blind.

Saint-Simon was a son of the great French Revolution, at the outbreak of which he was not yet 30. The Revolution was the victory of the third estate, ie, of the great masses of the nation, who were *active* in production and in trade, over the thus far privileged *idle* estates, the nobility and the clergy. But the victory of the third estate soon revealed itself as exclusively the victory of a small part of this estate, as the conquest of political power by its socially privileged stratum, ie, the propertied bourgeoisie. To be sure, the bourgeoisie had already developed rapidly during the Revolution, partly by speculation in the lands of the nobility and of the Church which had been confiscated and then *sold*, and partly by frauds on the nation by means of army contracts. It was precisely the domination of these swindlers that brought France and the Revolution to the verge of ruin under the Directorate, and thus gave Napoleon the pretext for his coup d'etat.

Hence in Saint-Simon's mind the antagonism between the third estate and the privileged estates took the form of an antagonism between 'workers' and 'idlers'. The idlers were not merely the old privileged persons, but also all who lived on their incomes without taking any part in production or distribution. The 'workers' were not only the wage workers, but also the manufacturers, the merchants, the bankers. That the idlers had lost the capacity for intellectual leadership and political supremacy had been proved and finally settled by the Revolution. That the non-possessing classes lacked this capacity seemed to Saint-Simon proved by the experiences of the Reign of Terror. Who then was to lead and command? According to Saint-Simon, science and industry, both united by a new religious bond destined to restore that unity of religious ideas which had been broken since the Reformation—a necessarily mystical and rigidly hierarchical 'new Christianity'. But science was the scholars; and industry was, in the first place, the active bourgeois, manufacturers, merchants, bankers. Of course, these bourgeois were to transform themselves into public officials, into trustees of society, of a sort; but they were still to hold a commanding and even economically privileged position vis-a-vis the workers. The bankers especially were to be called upon to direct the whole of social production by the regulation of credit. This conception was in exact keeping with a time when large scale industry and with it the chasm between bourgeoisie and proletariat were only just coming into existence in France. But what Saint-Simon especially lays stress on is this: what interests him first and above all other things is the lot of 'the largest and poorest class'.

In his *Letters from Geneva*, Saint-Simon already laid down the principle that 'all men ought to work'. In the same work he also recognised that the Reign of Terror was the reign of the propertyless masses. 'See,' he calls out to them, 'what happened in France at the time when your comrades held sway there; they brought about a famine.'[4]

But to recognise the French Revolution as a class struggle and not simply as one between nobility and bourgeoisie, but between nobility, bourgeoisie, *and those without any property*, was, in the year 1802, a discovery of the greatest genius. In 1816 he declared that politics was the science of production and foretold the complete absorption of politics by economics.[5] Although the knowledge that economic conditions are the basis of political institutions appears here only in embryo, what is already very plainly expressed is the transition from political rule over men to the administration of things and the guidance of the processes of production—that is to say, the 'abolition of the state', about which there has recently been so much noise. Saint-Simon showed the same superiority over his contemporaries, when in 1814, immediately after the entry of the Allies into Paris, and again in 1815, during the Hundred Days' War, he proclaimed the alliance of France with England, and then of both these countries with Germany, as the only guarantee for the prosperous development and peace of Europe.[6] To preach an alliance with the victors of Waterloo to the French in 1815 undoubtedly required as much courage as historical foresight.

If in Saint-Simon we find a masterly breadth of view, by virtue of which almost all the ideas of later socialists that are not strictly economic are found in him in embryo, we find in Fourier a criticism of the existing conditions of society which, while genuinely French and witty, is none the less penetrating. Fourier takes the bourgeoisie, their inspired prophets before the Revolution and their mercenary sycophants after it, at their own word. He mercilessly lays bare the material and moral misery of the bourgeois world. He confronts it with the earlier philosophers' dazzling promises of a society ruled solely by reason, of a civilisation yielding universal happiness, of an illimitable human perfectibility, as well as with the rose coloured phraseology of the bourgeois ideologists of his time. He shows how everywhere the most pitiful reality corresponds with the most high sounding phrases, and he overwhelms this hopeless fiasco of phrases with his mordant sarcasm.

Fourier is not only a critic; his eternal sprightliness makes him a satirist, and assuredly one of the greatest satirists of all time. He depicts with equal virtuosity and wit the swindling speculation that blossomed out on the downfall of the Revolution and the universal shopkeeping spirit of the French commerce of the time. Still more masterly is his criticism of the bourgeois form of the relations between the sexes and of the position of woman in bourgeois society. He was the first to declare that in any given society the degree of woman's emancipation is the natural measure of the general emancipation.[7]

But it is in his conception of the history of society that Fourier appears at his greatest. He divides its whole course thus far into four stages of development: savagery, the patriarchy, barbarism, and civilisation, the last coinciding with what is now called bourgeois society, ie, with the social order that came in with the sixteenth century.[8] He proves that 'the civilised order gives every vice practised by barbarism in a simple fashion a complex, ambiguous, equivocal, hypocritical form'; that civilisation moves in 'a vicious circle', in contradictions which it constantly reproduces without being able to solve, so that it constantly attains the opposite of what it wants to achieve, or pretends it wants to achieve. So that, for example, 'under civilisation *poverty is born of abundance itself*'.[9]

Fourier, as we see, handles dialectics with the same mastery as his contemporary Hegel. Using these same dialectics, he points out in opposition to the talk about illimitable human perfectibility that every historical era has its downward as well as upward phase, and he applies this way of looking at things to the future of the whole human race.[10] Just as Kant introduced the idea of the ultimate destruction of the earth into natural science, Fourier introduced that of the ultimate destruction of the human race into historical thought.

Whilst in France the hurricane of the Revolution swept over the land, in England a quieter but on that account no less mighty upheaval was taking place. Steam and the new tool making machinery were transforming manufacture into modern large scale industry and thus revolutionising the whole foundation of bourgeois society. The sluggish pace of development of the manufacturing period changed into a veritable period of storm and stress in production. The division of society into big capitalists and propertyless proletarians went on with ever increasing rapidity; between these, instead of the former stable middle estate, an unstable mass of artisans and small shopkeepers, which constituted the most fluctuating section of the population, now led a precarious existence.

The new mode of production was still only at the beginning of its upward phase; it was still the normal, regular mode of production—the only possible one under existing conditions. Nevertheless, even then it was producing crying social abuses—the herding together of a homeless population in the worst quarters of the large towns; the dissolution of all traditional bonds of descent, of patriarchal subordination, of the family; overwork, especially of women and children, on an appalling scale; massive demoralisation of the working class, suddenly flung into altogether new conditions, from the country into the town, from agriculture into industry, from stable conditions of existence into insecure ones changing from day to day.

At this juncture a 29 year old manufacturer came forward as a reformer—a man of almost sublime, child-like simplicity of character, and at the same time a born leader of men such as is rarely seen. Robert Owen had adopted the teaching of the materialist philosophers of the Enlightenment: that man's character is the product of his inherited constitution on the one hand, and of his environment during his lifetime, especially during his period of growth, on the other. In the Industrial Revolution most of his class saw only chaos and confusion, and the opportunity of fishing in troubled waters and getting rich quickly. He saw in it the opportunity of putting his favourite theory into practice, and so of bringing order out of chaos. He had already tried it out with success in Manchester, as the manager of a factory with 500 workers. From 1800 to 1829 he directed the great cotton spinning mill of New Lanark in Scotland as managing partner, along the same lines but with greater freedom of action, and with a success which won him a European reputation. He transformed a population, which originally consisted of the most diverse and for the most part very demoralised elements and which gradually grew to 2,500, into a model colony, in which drunkenness, police, magistrates, lawsuits, poor law relief and any need for charity were unknown. All this simply by placing the people in conditions more worthy of human beings, and especially by having the rising generation carefully brought up. He was the inventor of infant schools, and first introduced them at New Lanark. From the age of two the children came to school, where they enjoyed themselves so much that they could scarcely be got home again. Whilst his competitors worked their people 13 to 14 hours a day, in New Lanark the working day was only ten and a half hours. When a crisis in cotton stopped work for four months, his unemployed workers received their full wages all the time. Yet the business more than doubled in value, and to the last yielded large profits to its proprietors.

In spite of all this, Owen was not content. The existence he had contrived for his workers was, in his eyes, still far from being worthy of human beings. 'The people were slaves at my mercy.' The relatively favourable conditions in which he had placed them were still far from allowing an all-round rational development of the character and of the intellect, much less the free exercise of all their faculties.

And yet, the working part of this population of 7,500 persons was daily producing as much real wealth for society as, less than half a century before, it would have required the working part of a population of 600,000 to create. I asked myself, what became of the difference between the wealth consumed by 2,500 persons and that which would have been consumed by 600,000?[11]

The answer was clear. It had been used to pay the proprietors of the establishment 5 percent on their invested capital and in addition a profit of over £300,000. And that which held for New Lanark held to a still greater extent for all the factories in England.

If this new wealth had not been created by machinery,... the wars... in opposition to Napoleon and to support the aristocratic principles of society, could not have been maintained. And yet this new power was the creation of the working class.[12]

To the working class, therefore, the fruits belonged too. To Owen the newly created gigantic productive forces, which had hitherto served only to enrich individuals and to enslave the masses, offered the foundations for a reconstruction of society and were destined, as the common property of all, solely to work for the common good of all.

Owenite communism arose in this purely business way, as the outcome, so to speak, of commercial calculation. Throughout, it maintained this practical character. Thus, in 1823, Owen proposed the relief of the distress in Ireland by communist colonies, and drew up complete estimates of initial costs, yearly expenditure, and probable revenue.[13] Similarly, in his definitive plan for the future, the technical working out of details is managed with such practical knowledge—plan, elevation and bird's eye view all included—that, once the Owenite method of social reform is accepted, there is little to be said against the actual arrangement of details even from a specialist's point of view.

His advance in the direction of communism was the turning point in Owen's life. As long as he was simply a philanthropist, he was rewarded with nothing but wealth, applause, honour, and glory. He was the most popular man in Europe. Not only men of his own class, but statesmen and princes listened to him approvingly. But when he came out with his communist theories, it was quite a different story. Three great obstacles seemed to him especially to block the path to social reform: private property, religion, and marriage in its present form. He knew what confronted him if he attacked them—universal ostracism by official society and the loss of his whole social standing. But nothing of this prevented him from attacking them without fear of the consequences, and what he had foreseen came to pass. Banished from official society, with a conspiracy of silence against him in the press, and ruined by his unsuccessful communist experiments in America in which he sacrificed all his fortune, he turned directly to the working class and continued working in their midst for 30 years. Every social movement, every real advance in England on behalf of the workers is linked with Owen's name. Thus in 1819, after five years' effort he pushed through the first law limiting the labour of women and children in factories.[14] He presided over the first congress at which all the trade unions of England united in a single great trade union association.[15] He introduced as transition measures to the complete communist organisation of society, on the one hand, co-operative societies (both consumers' and producers'), which have since at least given practical proof that the merchant and the manufacturer are quite superfluous personages. On the other hand, he introduced labour bazaars for the exchange of the products of labour through the medium of labour notes with the labour hour as the unit; institutions necessarily doomed to failure, but completely anticipating the much later Proudhon exchange bank, and differing only from the latter in that they did not claim to be the panacea for all social ills, but just a first step towards a much more radical transformation of society.[16]

The Utopians' outlook has governed the socialist ideas of the nineteenth century for a long time and in part still does. Until very recently all French and English socialists paid homage to it. The earlier German communism, including that of Weitling, also belongs to it. To all these socialism is the expression of absolute truth, reason and justice and needs only to be discovered to conquer the world by virtue of its own power; as absolute truth is independent of time, space, and human historical development, it is a mere accident when and where it is discovered. At the same time, absolute truth, reason and justice are different for the founder of each different school; and as each one's special brand of absolute truth, reason and justice is in turn conditioned by his subjective understanding, his conditions of existence, the measure of his knowledge and his intellectual training, there is no other ending possible in this conflict of absolute truths than that they should grind each other down. Hence, from this nothing could come but a kind of eclectic, average socialism, such as in fact has dominated the minds of most of the socialist workers in France and England up to the present time; a mish-mash permitting of the most manifold shades of opinion; a mish-mash of the less striking critical statements, economic theories and pictures of future society of the founders of different sects; a mish-mash which is the more easily produced, the more the sharp edges of precision of the individual constituents are rubbed down in the stream of debate, like rounded pebbles in a brook. To make a science of socialism, it had first to be placed upon a real basis.

Chapter 2

IN THE meantime, the new German philosophy, terminating in Hegel, had arisen along with and after the French philosophy of the eighteenth century. Its greatest merit was its resumption of dialectics as the highest form of thinking. The old Greek philosophers were all born dialecticians, and Aristotle, the most encyclopaedic intellect among them, had already investigated the most essential forms of dialectical thought. On the other hand, although the newer philosophy, too, included brilliant exponents of dialectics (eg, Descartes and Spinoza), it had become—especially under English influence—increasingly stuck in the so-called metaphysical mode of reasoning, by which the French of the eighteenth century were also almost wholly dominated, at all events in their special philosophical works. Outside philosophy in the narrow sense, the French nevertheless produced masterpieces of dialectic; we need only call to mind Diderot's *Rameau's Nephew* and Rousseau's *Discourse on the Origin of Inequality Among Men*.[1] We give here, in brief, the essential character of these two modes of thought.

When we reflect on nature or the history of

mankind or our own intellectual activity, at first we see the picture of an endless maze of connections and interactions, in which nothing remains what, where and as it was, but everything moves, changes, comes into being and passes away. At first, therefore, we see the picture as a whole, with its individual parts still more or less kept in the background; we observe the movements, transitions, connections, rather than *the things* that move, change and are connected. This primitive, naive, but intrinsically correct conception of the world is that of ancient Greek philosophy, and was first clearly formulated by Heraclitus: everything is and also is not, for everything is *in flux*, is constantly changing, constantly coming into being and passing away.

But this conception, correctly as it expresses the general character of the picture of phenomena as a whole, does not suffice to explain the details of which this picture is made up, and so long as we do not know these, we are not clear about the whole picture. In order to understand these details we must detach them from their natural or historical connection and examine each one separately according to its nature, special causes and effects, etc. This is primarily the task of natural science and historical research, branches of science which for the Greeks of classical times occupied only a subordinate position on very good grounds, because they had first of all to piece together the materials for these sciences to work upon. Only after a certain amount of natural and historical material has been collected can critical analysis, comparison, and arrangement in classes, orders, and species be undertaken. The beginnings of the exact natural sciences were, therefore, worked out first by the Greeks of the Alexandrian period, and later on, in the Middle Ages, further developed by the Arabs.[2] Genuine natural science dates from the second half of the fifteenth century, and from then on it has advanced with ever increasing rapidity. The analysis of nature into its individual parts, the division of the different natural processes and objects into definite classes, the study of the internal anatomy of organic bodies in their manifold forms—these were the fundamental conditions for the gigantic strides in our knowledge of nature that have been made during the last 400 years. But this has bequeathed us the habit of observing natural objects and processes in isolation, detached from the general context; of observing them not in their motion, but in their state of rest; not as essentially variable elements, but as constant ones; not in their life, but in their death. And when this way of looking at things was transferred by Bacon and Locke from natural science to philosophy, it begot the narrow, metaphysical mode of thought peculiar to the last centuries.

To the metaphysician, things and their mental images, ideas, are isolated, to be considered one after the other and apart from each other, fixed, rigid objects of investigation given once for all. He thinks in absolutely unmediated antitheses. 'His communication is "yea, yea; nay, nay"; for whatsoever is more than these cometh of evil.' For him a thing either exists or does not exist; a thing cannot at the same time be itself and something else. Positive and negative absolutely exclude one another; cause and effect stand in a rigid antithesis one to the other.

At first sight this way of thinking seems to us most plausible because it is that of so-called sound common sense. Yet sound common sense, respectable fellow that he is in the homely realm of his own four walls, has very wonderful adventures directly he ventures out into the wide world of research. The metaphysical mode of thought, justifiable and even necessary as it is in a number of domains whose extent varies according to the nature of the object, invariably bumps into a limit sooner or later, beyond which it becomes one sided, restricted, abstract, lost in insoluble contradictions, because in the presence of individual things it forgets their connections; because in the presence of their existence it forgets their coming into being and passing away; because in their state of rest it forgets their motion. It cannot see the wood for the trees. For everyday purposes we know and can definitely say, eg, whether an animal is alive or not. But, upon closer inquiry, we find that this is sometimes a very complex question, as the jurists very well know. They have cudgelled their brains in vain to discover a rational limit beyond which the killing of the child in its mother's womb is murder. It is just as impossible to determine the moment of death, for physiology proves that death is not a sudden instantaneous phenomenon, but a very protracted process.

In like manner, every organic being is every moment the same and not the same; every moment it assimilates matter supplied from without and gets rid of other matter; every moment some cells of its body die and others build themselves anew; in a longer or shorter time the matter of its body is completely renewed and is replaced by other molecules of matter, so that every organic being is always itself, and yet something other than itself.

Further, we find upon closer investigation that the two poles of an antithesis, like positive and negative, are as inseparable as they are opposed, and that despite all their opposition, they interpenetrate. In like manner, we find that cause and effect are conceptions which only hold good in their application to the individual case as such; but as soon as we consider the individual case in its general connection with the universe as a whole, they merge, they dissolve in the concept of universal action and reaction in which causes and effects are constantly changing places, so that what is effect here and now will be cause there and then, and vice versa.

None of these processes and modes of thought fit into the frame of metaphysical thinking. But for dialectics, which grasps things and their conceptual images essentially in their interconnection, in their concatenation, their motion, their coming into and passing out of existence, such processes as those mentioned above are so many corroborations of its own procedure.

Nature is the test of dialectics, and it must be said for modern science that it has furnished this test with very rich and daily increasing materials, and thus has shown that in the last resort nature works dialectically and not metaphysically; that she does not move in an eternally uniform and perpetually recurring circle, but goes through a genuine historical evolution. In this connection Darwin must be named before all others. He dealt the metaphysical conception of nature the heaviest blow by his proof that the organic world of today—plants, animals, and consequently man too—is the product of a process of evolution going on through millions of years. But since the natural scientists who have learned to think dialectically are still few and far between, this conflict of the results of discovery with traditional modes of thinking explains the endless confusion now reigning in theoretical natural science, the despair of teachers as well as students, of authors and readers alike.

An exact representation of the universe, of its evolution and of that of mankind, and of the reflection of this evolution in the minds of men can therefore only be obtained by the method of dialectics with its constant regard to the general actions and reactions of becoming and ceasing to be, of progressive or retrogressive changes. And it is in this spirit that modern German philosophy immediately set to work. Kant began his career by resolving the stable solar system of Newton and its eternal duration, after the famous initial impulse had once been given, into a historical process, the formation of the sun and all the planets out of a rotating nebulous mass. From this he already drew the conclusion that, given this origin of the solar system, its future death followed of necessity. Half a century later his theory was established mathematically by Laplace, and after another half century the spectroscope confirmed the existence in cosmic space of such incandescent masses of gas in various stages of condensation.

This new German philosophy terminated in the Hegelian system. In this system—and this is its great merit—the whole world, natural, historical, intellectual, is for the first time represented as a process, ie, as in constant motion, change, transformation, development; and the attempt was made to show internal interconnections in this motion and development. From this point of view the history of mankind no longer appeared as a wild whirl of senseless deeds of violence, all equally condemnable at the judgment seat of mature philosophic reason and best forgotten as quickly as possible, but as the process of evolution of humanity itself. It was now the task of the intellect to follow the gradual march of this process through all its devious ways, and to trace out the inner logic running through all its apparently contingent phenomena.

That the Hegelian system did not solve the problem it posed itself is immaterial here. Its epoch-making merit was that it posed the problem. This problem is indeed one that no single individual will ever be able to solve. Although Hegel was—with Saint-Simon—the most encyclopaedic mind of his time, he was restricted, first, by the necessarily limited extent of his own knowledge and, second, by the limited extent and depth of the knowledge and conceptions of his epoch. To these limits a third must be added. Hegel was an idealist. To him the thoughts within his brain were not the more or less abstract images of actual things and processes, but on the contrary, things and their development were only the realised images of the 'Idea', existing somehow from eternity before the world existed. Consequently everything was stood on its head and the actual interconnection of things in the world was completely reversed. Although Hegel had grasped some individual interconnections correctly and with genius, yet for the reasons just given there is much that in point of detail necessarily turned out botched, artificial, laboured, in a word, upside down. The Hegelian system as such was a colossal miscarriage—but it was also the last of its kind. In fact, it was suffering from an internal and incurable contradition. On the one hand, its essential postulate was the conception that human history is a process of development, which, by its very nature, cannot find its intellectual final term in the discovery of any so-called absolute truth. But on the other hand, it laid claim to being the very essence of precisely this absolute truth. A system of natural and historical knowledge which is all-embracing and final for all time is in contradiction with the fundamental laws of dialectical thinking; which by no means excludes, but on the contrary includes, the idea that systematic knowledge of the entire external world can make giant strides from generation to generation.

The recognition of the complete inversion of previous German idealism necessarily led to materialism, but, it must be noted, not to the purely metaphysical, exclusively mechanical materialism of the eighteenth century. In contrast to the naively revolutionary, flat rejection of all previous history, modern materialism sees history as the process of development of humanity and its own task as the discovery of the laws of motion of this process. The conception was prevalent among the French of the eighteenth century and later in Hegel that nature was a whole, moving in narrow circles and for ever remaining immutable, with eternal celestial bodies, as in Newton's teaching, and with unalterable species of organic beings, as in Linnaeus' teaching. In opposition to this conception, modern materialism embraces the more recent advances of natural science, according to which nature too has its history in time, the celestial bodies, like the organic species with which they became peopled under favourable conditions, coming into being and passing away, and the recurrent cycles, insofar as they are at all admissible, assuming infinitely vaster dimensions. In both cases modern materialism is essentially dialectical and no longer needs any philosophy standing above the other sciences. As soon as each separate science is required to clarify its position in the great totality of things and of our knowledge of things, a special science dealing with this totality is superfluous. All that remains in an independent state from all earlier philosophy is the science of thought and its laws—formal logic and dialectics. Everything else merges into the positive science of nature and history.

But whilst the revolution in the conception of nature could only be made to the extent that research furnished the corresponding positive materials, certain historical events had already asserted themselves much earlier which led to a decisive change in the conception of history. In 1831, the first working class rising took place in Lyons; between 1838 and 1842, the first national working class movement, that of the English Chartists, reached its height. The class struggle between proletariat and bourgeoisie came to the front in the history of the most advanced countries in Europe in proportion to the development, on the one hand, of modern industry, and on the other, of the recently acquired political supremacy of the bourgeoisie. Facts more and more strenuously gave the lie to the teachings of bourgeois economics on the identity of the interests of capital and labour, on the general harmony and general prosperity flowing from free competition. None of these things could be ignored any longer, any more than the French and English socialism, which was their theoretical, though extremely imperfect, expression. But the old idealist conception of history, which was not yet dislodged, knew nothing of class struggles based on material interests, indeed knew nothing at all of material interests; production and all economic relations appeared in it only as incidental, subordinate elements in the 'history of civilisation'.

The new facts made imperative a new examination of all past history. Then it was seen that *all* past history, with the exception of its primitive stages, was the history of class struggles; that these social classes warring with each other are always the products of the relations of production and exchange— in a word, of the *economic* relations of their epoch; that therefore the economic structure of society always forms the real basis, from which, in the last analysis, the whole superstructure of legal and political institutions as well as of the religious, philosophical, and other ideas of a given historical period is to be explained. Hegel had freed the conception of history from metaphysics—he had made it dialectical; but his conception of history was essentially idealistic. But now idealism was driven from its last refuge, the conception of history; now a materialistic treatment of history was advanced, and the way found to explain man's consciousness by his being, instead of, as heretofore, his being by his consciousness.

Henceforward socialism no longer appeared as an accidental discovery by this or that intellect of genius, but as the necessary outcome of the struggle between two classes produced by history—the proletariat and the bourgeoisie. Its task was no longer to manufacture as perfect a system of society as possible, but to examine the historico-economic process from which these classes and their antagonism had of necessity sprung and to discover in the economic situation thus created the means of ending the conflict. But the earlier socialism was just as incompatible with this materialist conception of history as the French materialists' conception of nature was with dialectics and modern natural science. The earlier socialism certainly criticised the existing capitalist mode of production and its consequences. But it could not explain this mode of production, and, therefore, could not get the mastery of it. It could only simply reject it as evil. The more violently it denounced the exploitation of the working class, which is inseparable from capitalism, the less able was it clearly to show in what this exploitation consists and how it arises. But for this it was necessary, on the one hand, to present the capitalist mode of production in its historical interconnection and its necessity for a specific historical period, and therefore also the necessity of its doom; and, on the other, to lay bare its essential character, which was still hidden. This was done by the discovery of *surplus value*. It was shown that the appropriation of unpaid labour is the basic form of the capitalist mode of production and of the exploitation of the worker effected by it; that even if the capitalist buys the labour power of his worker at the full value it possesses as a commodity on the market, he still extracts more value from it than he paid for; and that in the last analysis this surplus value forms those sums of value from which there is heaped up the constantly increasing mass of capital in the hands of the possessing classes. The process both of capitalist production and of the production of capital was explained.

These two great discoveries, the materialist conception of history and the revelation of the secret of capitalist production through surplus value, we owe to *Marx*. With them socialism became a science, which had now to be elaborated in all its details and interconnections.

Chapter 3

THE MATERIALIST conception of history starts from the principle that production and, next to production, the exchange of things produced, is the basis of every social order; that in every society that has appeared in history, the distribution of wealth and with it the division of society into classes or estates are dependent upon what is produced, how it is produced, and how the products are exchanged. Accordingly, the ultimate causes of all social changes and political revolutions are to be sought, not in men's brains, not in their growing insight into eternal truth and justice, but in changes in the modes of production and exchange. They are to be sought, not in the *philosophy*, but in the *economics* of each particular epoch. The growing recognition that existing social institutions are irrational and unjust, that reason has become unreason, and kindness a scourge, is only a sign that changes in the modes of production and exchange have silently been taking place with which the social order adapted to earlier economic conditions is no longer in keeping. From this it also follows that the means of eliminating the abuses that have been brought to light must also be present, in a more or less developed condition, within the changed relations of production themselves. These means are not to be *invented* out of one's brain, but *discovered* by the brain in the existing material facts of production.

Where, then, does modern socialism stand?

It is now pretty generally conceded that the existing social order is the creation of the ruling class of today, of the bourgeoisie. The mode of production peculiar to the bourgeoisie, which since Marx has been called the capitalist mode of production, was incompatible with the local privileges and the privileges of estate as well as with the reciprocal personal ties of the feudal system. The bourgeoisie shattered the feudal system and on its ruins built the bourgeois social order, the realm of free competition, of freedom of movement, of equal rights for commodity owners and all the glories of capitalism. The capitalist mode of production could now develop freely. Since steam and the new tool making machinery transformed the older manufacture into large scale industry, the productive forces evolved under the guidance of the bourgeoisie developed with a rapidity and on a scale unheard of before. But just as manufacture and the handicraft industries, which had experienced a further growth under its influence, had come into conflict with the feudal trammels of the guilds in their time, so large scale industry, in its more complete development, now comes into conflict with the barriers within which the capitalist mode of production holds it confined. The new productive forces have already outgrown the bourgeois form of using them; and this conflict between productive forces and mode of production is not a conflict engendered in men's heads, like that between original sin and divine justice, but it exists in the

88

facts, objectively, outside us, independently of the will and even actions of the men who have brought it on. Modern socialism is nothing but the reflex in thought of this actual conflict, its ideal reflection in the minds of above all the class directly suffering under it, the working class.

Now, in what does this conflict consist?

Prior to capitalist production, ie, in the Middle Ages, small scale production generally prevailed, based upon the workers' private ownership of their means of production: the agriculture of the small peasant, freeman or serf, and the handicrafts in the towns. The instruments of labour—land, agricultural implements, the workshop, the hand tool—were the instruments of labour of single individuals, adapted for individual use, and, therefore, of necessity puny, dwarfish, circumscribed. But for this very reason they normally belonged to the producer himself. To concentrate these scattered, limited means of production, to enlarge them, to turn them into the powerful levers of production of the present day was precisely the historic role of the capitalist mode of production and of its upholder, the bourgeoisie. In Part IV of *Capital* Marx gives a detailed account of how the bourgeoisie has historically accomplished this since the fifteenth century through the three phases of simple co-operation, manufacture and large scale industry. But as is also shown there, the bourgeoisie could not transform these limited means of production into mighty productive forces without at the same time transforming them from individual means of production into *social* means of production only workable by a *collectivity of men*. The spinning wheel, the hand loom and the blacksmith's hammer were replaced by the spinning machine, the power loom and the steam hammer, and the individual workshop by the factory commanding the co-operation of hundreds and thousands of workmen. Like the means of production, production itself changed from a series of individual operations into a series of social acts, and the products from individual into social products. The yarn, the cloth and the metal goods that now came out of the factory were the common product of many workers, through whose hands they had successively to pass before they were ready. No one person could say of them: '*I* made that, this is *my* product.'

But where the spontaneous division of labour within society, a division of labour which arose gradually and planlessly, is the fundamental form of production, it imprints on the products the form of *commodities*, the mutual exchange, purchase and sale of which enable the individual producers to satisfy their manifold wants. This was the case in the Middle Ages. The peasant, for example, sold the artisan agricultural products and bought from him the products of his craft. The new mode of production infiltrated this society of individual producers, of commodity producers. It set up the *planned* division of labour, as it was organised in the individual factory, in the midst of the spontaneous, *planless* division of labour such as then prevailed throughout society; side by side with *individual* production, *social* production made its appearance. The products of both were sold in the same market, and, consequently, at the same prices, at least approximately. But planned organisation was stronger than the spontaneous division of labour; the factories working socially produced their commodities more cheaply than the isolated small producers. Individual production succumbed in one field after another. Social production totally revolutionised the old mode of production. But this, its revolutionary, character was so little recognised that it was, on the contrary, introduced as a means of increasing and promoting commodity production. In its origin, it was directly tied up with certain already existing levers of commodity production and exchange: merchant capital, handicrafts, wage labour. Since social production itself appeared as a new form of commodity production, the old forms of appropriation characteristic of commodity production remained in full force for it too.

In commodity production as it had developed in the Middle Ages, any question concerning the identity of the owner of the product of labour just couldn't arise. The individual producer had generally produced it from his own raw material, which was often his own handiwork, with his own instruments of labour, and by his own or his family's manual labour. There was no need whatever for him to appropriate the product to begin with, it belonged to him wholly as a matter of course. His ownership of the product was therefore based *upon his own labour*. Even where outside help was used, it was generally of little importance, and often received other compensation in addition to wages; the guild apprentice and journeyman worked less for board and wages than for training to become master craftsmen themselves.

Then came the concentration of the means of production in large workshops and manufactories, their transformation into actual social means of production. But the social means of production and products were treated as if they were still the means of production and the products of individuals they had been before. Hitherto, the owner of the instruments of labour had appropriated the product, because it was normally his own product and the auxiliary labour of others was the exception. Now the owner of the instruments of labour continued to appropriate the product, although it was no longer *his* product, but exclusively the product of the *labour of others*. Thus, the products which were now turned out socially were not appropriated by those who had actually set the means of production in motion and actually turned out the products, but by the *capitalists*. The means of production and production itself have become social in essence. But they are subjected to a form of appropriation which presupposes private production by individuals, and under which, therefore, everyone owns his own product and brings it to market. The mode of production is subjected to this form of appropriation, although it removes the presupposition on which the latter rests.[1] *The whole conflict of today is already present in embryo* in this contradiction which gives the new mode of production its capitalist character. The more the new mode of production became dominant in all decisive fields of production and in all economically decisive countries, and the more it reduced individual production to an insignificant residue, *the more glaring did the incompatibility of social production with capitalist appropriation necessarily become*.

As we have said, the first capitalists found the form of wage labour already in existence. But wage labour as the exception, as a side occupation, as an auxiliary, as a transitory phase. The agricultural labourer who occasionally went to work as a day labourer had a few acres of his own land, from which alone he could get his living in a pinch. The regulations of the guilds ensured that the journeyman of today became the master craftsman of tomorrow. But this changed as soon as the means of production became social and were concentrated in the hands of capitalists. Both the means of production and the products of the small individual producer increasingly depreciated in value; there was nothing left for him to do but to go to the capitalist and work for wages. From being an exception and an auxiliary, wage labour became the rule and the basic form of all production; from being a side occupation, it now became the worker's exclusive activity. The occasional wage worker was transformed into the wage worker for life. Furthermore, the number of lifelong wage workers was enormously increased by the simultaneous collapse of the feudal system, the disbanding of the feudal lords' retainers, the eviction of peasants from their homesteads, etc. The separation of the means of production concentrated in the hands of the capitalists, on the one side, from the producers now possessing nothing but their labour power, on the other, was accomplished. *The contradiction between social production and capitalist appropriation became manifest as the antagonism between proletariat and bourgeoisie.*

We have seen that the capitalist mode of production infiltrated a society of commodity producers, individual producers, whose social nexus was mediated through the exchange of their products. But every society based on commodity production has the peculiarity that the producers in it have lost command over their own social relations. Each produces for himself with the means of production which happen to be at his disposal and in order to satisfy his individual needs through exchange. No one knows how much of the article he produces is coming onto the market or how much will be wanted, no one knows whether his individual product will meet a real need, whether he will cover his costs or even be able to sell it at all. Anarchy of social production prevails. But like all other forms of production, commodity production has its own peculiar laws, which are inherent in and inseparable from it; and these laws assert themselves despite anarchy, in and through anarchy. They are manifested in the only persistent form of the social nexus, in exchange, and impose themselves on the individual producers as compulsory laws of competition. At first, therefore, they are unknown to these producers themselves and have to be discovered by them gradually, only through long experience. Thus they assert themselves without the producers and against the producers, as the natural laws of their form of production, working blindly. The product dominates the producers.

In mediaeval society, especially in the earlier centuries, production was essentially for the producer's own use. In the main it only satisfied the wants of the producer and his family. Where personal relations of dependence existed as in the countryside, it also contributed towards satisfying the wants of the feudal lord. No exchange was involved here, and consequently the products did not assume the character of commodities. The peasant family produced almost everything it required—utensils and clothing as well as food. It was only when it succeeded in producing a surplus beyond its own wants and the payments in kind due to the feudal lord—it was only at this stage that it also produced commodities; this surplus thrown into social exchange and offered for sale became a commodity. The town artisans, it is true, had to produce for exchange from the very beginning. But they too covered the greatest part of their own wants themselves; they had gardens and small fields; they sent their cattle out into the communal woodland, which also provided them with timber and firewood; the women spun flax, wool, etc. Production for the purpose of exchange, the production of commodities, was only just coming into being. Hence, restricted exchange, restricted market, stable mode of production, local isolation from the outside world, and local unity within: the Mark in the countryside, the guild in the town.

But with the extension of commodity production and especially with the emergence of the capitalist mode of production, the previously dormant laws of commodity production began to operate more openly and more potently. The old bonds were loosened, the old dividing barriers were broken through, the producers were more and more transformed into independent, isolated producers of commodities. The anarchy of social production became obvious and was carried to further and further extremes. But the chief means by which the capitalist mode of production accentuated this anarchy in social production was the exact opposite of anarchy—the increasing organisation of production as social production in each individual productive establishment. With this lever it put an end to the old peaceful stability. In whatever branch of industry it was introduced, it suffered no older method of operation alongside it; wherever it laid hold of a handicraft, it wiped the old handicraft out. The field of labour became a field of battle. The great geographical discoveries and the colonisation which followed on them multiplied markets and hastened the transformation of handicraft into manufacture. The struggle broke out not only between the individual local producers; in turn the local struggles grew into national struggles, the commercial wars of the seventeenth and eighteenth centuries. Finally, large scale industry and the creation of the world market have made the struggle universal and at the same time given it an unparalleled virulence. Between individual capitalists, as between whole industries and whole countries, advantages in natural or artificial conditions of production decide life or death. The vanquished are relentlessly cast aside. It is the Darwinian struggle for individual existence, transferred from nature to society with a fury raised to the n-th power. The brutish state of nature appears as the peak of human development. The contradiction between social production and capitalist appropriation reproduces itself as the *antagonism between the organisation of production in the individual factory and the anarchy of production in society as a whole*.

The capitalist mode of production moves in these two phenomenal forms of the contradiction immanent in it by its very origin, it relentlessly describes that 'vicious circle' which Fourier had already discovered. But what Fourier in his day was as yet unable to see is that this circle is gradually narrowing, that the motion is rather in the form of a spiral and must come to an end, like the motion of the planets, by collision with the centre. It is the motive force of the social anarchy of production which increasingly transforms the great majority of men into proletarians, and it is the proletarian masses in their turn who will ultimately put an end to the anarchy of production. It is the motive force of the social anarchy of production which transforms the infinite perfectibility of the machine in large scale industry into a compulsory commandment for each individual industrial capitalist to make his machinery more and more perfect, under penalty of ruin.

But the perfecting of machinery means rendering human labour superfluous. If the introduction and increase of machinery meant the displacement of millions of hand workers by a few machine workers, the improvement of machinery means the displacement of larger and larger numbers of machine workers themselves, and ultimately the creation of a mass of available wage workers exceeding the average employment needs of capital, a complete industrial reserve army, as I called it as long ago as 1845,[2] an army available at times when industry is working at high pressure, to be thrown out onto the streets by the inevitable ensuing crash, a constant dead weight on the feet of the working class in its struggle for existence with capital, a regulator to keep wages down to the low level which suits the needs of capital. Thus it comes about that machinery, to use Marx's phrase, becomes the most powerful weapon in the war of capital against the working class, that the instruments of labour constantly knock the means of subsistence out of the worker's hands, that the very product of the worker is turned into an instrument for his enslavement. Thus it comes about that from the very beginning economy in the instruments of labour becomes at once the most reckless squandering of labour power and robbery committed against the normal conditions requisite for the labour function; that machinery, the most powerful means for shortening labour time, is converted into the most unfailing means for transforming the entire span of life of the worker and his family into disposable labour time for the purpose of expanding the value of capital.[3]

Thus it comes about that the overwork of some becomes the precondition for the unemployment of others and that large scale industry, which hunts the whole world over for new consumers, confines the consumption of the masses at home to a starvation minimum and thus undermines its own internal market. 'The law that always equilibriates the relative surplus population, or industrial reserve army, to the extent and energy of accumulation, this law rivets the labourer to capital more firmly than the wedges of Vulcan did Prometheus to the rock. It involves an accumulation of misery corresponding to the accumulation of capital. Accumulation of wealth at one pole is, therefore, at the same time accumulation of misery, agony of toil, slavery, ignorance, bestialisation, moral degradation, at the opposite pole, ie, on the side of the class that *produces its own product as capital.*'[4] To expect any other distribution of the products from the capitalist mode of production is like expecting the electrodes of a battery not to decompose water, not to develop oxygen at the positive pole and hydrogen at the negative, so long as they are connected with the battery.

We have seen how the capacity for improvement of modern machinery, which is pushed to a maximum, is transformed by the anarchy of social production into a compulsory commandment for the individual industrial capitalist constantly to improve his machinery, constantly to increase its productive power. The bare factual possibility of extending his field of production is transformed into a similar compulsory commandment for him. The enormous expansive force of large scale industry, compared to which that of gases is mere child's play, now appears to us as a need for qualitative and quantitative expansion that laughs at all counteracting pressure. Such counteracting pressure is formed by consumption, by sales, by markets for the products of large scale industry. But the capacity of the market to expand, both extensively and intensively, is primarily governed by quite different laws which operate far less energetically. The expansion of the market cannot keep pace with the expansion of production. The collision becomes inevitable, and since it can yield no solution so long as it does not burst the capitalist mode of production itself, it becomes periodic. Capitalist production generates a new 'vicious circle'.

In fact, since 1825, when the first general crisis erupted, the whole industrial and commercial world, production and exchange among all civilised peoples and their more or less barbarian appendages, have broken down about once every ten years. Trade comes to a standstill, markets are glutted, products lie around in piles as massive as they are unsaleable, hard cash disappears, credit vanishes, factories are idle, the working masses lack the means of subsistence because they have produced too much of them, bankruptcy follows upon bankruptcy, forced sale upon forced sale. The stagnation lasts for years, and both productive forces and products are squandered and destroyed wholesale, until the accumulated masses of commodities are finally run down at a more or less considerable depreciation and until production and exchange gradually begin to move again. By degrees the pace quickens, it becomes a trot, the industrial trot passes into a gallop, and the gallop in turn passes into the unbridled onrush of a complete industrial, commercial, credit and speculative steeplechase, only to end up again, after the most breakneck jumps—in the ditch of a crash. And so on over and over again. We have now experienced it fully five times since 1825, and at this moment (1877) we are experiencing it for the sixth time. The character of these crises is so clearly marked that Fourier hit them all off when he described the first as a *crise pléthorique*, a crisis of superabundance.

In these crises, the contradiction between social production and capitalist appropriation ends in a violent explosion. The circulation of commodities is for the moment reduced to nothing; money, the means of circulation, becomes an obstacle to circulation; all the laws of commodity production and commodity circulation are turned upside down. The economic collision has reached its culminating point: *the mode of production rebels against the mode of exchange*.

The fact that the social organisation of production within the factory has developed to the point at which it has become incompatible with the anarchy of production in society which exists side by side with and above it—this fact is made palpable to the capitalists themselves by the forcible concentration of capitals which takes place during crises through the ruin of many big and even more small capitalists. The whole mechanism of the capitalist mode of production breaks down under the pressure of the productive forces which it itself has created.

It is no longer able to transform the whole of this mass of means of production into capital; they lie idle, and for this very reason the industrial reserve army must also lie idle. Means of production, means of subsistence, available workers, all the elements of production and of general wealth are there in abundance. But 'abundance becomes the source of distress and want' (Fourier), because it is precisely abundance that prevents the conversion of the means of production and subsistence into capital. For in capitalist society the means of production cannot begin to function unless they have first been converted into capital, into means for the exploitation of human labour power. The necessity for the means of production and subsistence to take the character of capital stands like a ghost between them and the workers. It alone prevents the coming together of the material and personal levers of production; it alone forbids the means of production to function and the workers to work and to live. Thus on the one hand the capitalist mode of production stands convicted of its own incapacity to continue the administration of these productive forces. On the other hand, these productive forces themselves press forward with increasing power towards the abolition of the contradiction, to their deliverance from their character as capital, *towards the actual recognition of their character as social productive forces*.

It is this counter-pressure of the productive forces, in their mighty upgrowth, against their character as capital, this increasingly compulsive drive for the recognition of their social nature, which forces the capitalist class itself to treat them more and more as social productive forces, as far as this is at all possible within the framework of capitalist relations.

The period of industrial boom with its unlimited credit inflation no less than the crash itself operating through the collapse of large capitalist establishments, drives towards that form of the socialisation of larger masses of means of production which we find in the various kinds of joint stock companies. Many of these means of production and communication are so colossal from the outset that, like the railways, they exclude all other forms of capitalist exploitation. At a certain stage of development this form, too, no longer suffices; the large scale producers in one and the same branch of industry in a country unite in a 'trust', an association for the purpose of regulating production. They determine the total amount to be produced, parcel it out among themselves and thus enforce the selling price fixed beforehand. Since such trusts usually go to pieces as soon as business becomes bad, for this very reason they push towards a still more concentrated socialisation. The whole branch of industry is converted into one big joint stock company, and internal competition gives place to the internal monopoly of this one company; this happened as early as 1890 with English alkali production, which, after the fusion of all the 48 large works, is now carried on by a single company, under centralised direction, with a capital of £6 million.

In the trusts, free competition changes into monopoly and the planless production of capitalist society capitulates before the planned production of the invading socialist society. Of course, this is initially still to the benefit of the capitalists. But the exploitation becomes so palpable here that it must break down. No nation would put up with production directed by trusts, with such a barefaced exploitation of the community by a small band of coupon clippers.

In one way or another, with trusts or without, the state, the official representative of capitalist society, is finally constrained to take over the direction of production.[5] This necessity for conversion into state property first appears in the big communication organisations: the postal service, telegraphs and railways.

If the crises revealed the bourgeoisie's incapacity to continue to administer the modern productive forces, the conversion of the large production and communication establishments into joint stock companies, trusts and state property shows that the bourgeoisie can be dispensed with for this purpose. All the social functions of the capitalist are now conducted by salaried employees. The capitalist no longer has any social activity save the pocketing of revenues, the clipping of coupons and gambling on the stock exchange, where the different capitalists fleece each other of their capital. Just as at first the capitalist mode of production displaced the workers, so now it is displacing the capitalists, relegating them, just as it did the workers, to the superfluous population, although not immediately to the industrial reserve army.

But neither conversion into joint stock companies and trusts nor conversion into state property deprives the productive forces of their character as capital. This is obvious in the case of joint stock companies and trusts. But the modern state, too, is only the organisation with which bourgeois society provides itself in order to maintain the general external conditions of the capitalist mode of production against encroachments either by the workers or by individual capitalists. The modern state, whatever its form, is an essentially capitalist machine, the state of the capitalists, the ideal aggregate capitalist. The more productive forces it takes over into its possession, the more it becomes a real aggregate capitalist, the more citizens it exploits. The workers remain wage workers, proletarians. The capitalist relationship is not abolished, rather it is pushed to the limit. But at this limit it changes into its opposite. State ownership of the productive forces is not the solution of the conflict, but it contains within itself the formal means, the handle to the solution.

This solution can only consist in actually recognising the social nature of the modern productive forces and in therefore bringing the mode of production, appropriation and exchange into harmony with the social character of the means of production. This can only be brought about by society's openly and straightforwardly taking possession of the productive forces, which have outgrown all guidance other than that of society itself. Thus the social character of the means of production and of the products, which today reacts against the producers themselves, periodically ruptures the mode of production and exchange, and enforces itself only as a law of nature working blindly, violently and destructively, will be quite consciously asserted by the producers, and instead of being a source of disorder and periodic collapse will change into the most powerful lever of production itself.

The forces operating in society work exactly like the forces of nature—blindly, violently and destructively, so long as we fail to understand them and take them into account. But once we have recognised them and understood their action, their trend and their effects, it depends solely on ourselves to increasingly subject them to our will and to attain our ends through them. This is especially true of the mighty productive forces of the present day. As long as we obstinately refuse to understand their nature and their character—and the capitalist mode of production and its defenders resist such understanding with might and main—these forces operate in spite of us and against us, dominate us, as we have shown in detail. But once their nature is grasped, they can be transformed from demoniacal masters into willing servants in the hands of the producers working in association. It is the difference between the destructive force of electricity in the lightning of a thunderstorm and the tamed electricity of the telegraph and the arc light, the difference between a conflagration and fire working in the service of man. With this treatment of the present day productive forces according to their nature, which is now at last understood, a socially planned regulation of production in accordance with the needs of the community and of each individual takes the place of the anarchy of social production. The capitalist mode of appropriation, in which the product enslaves first the producer and then the appropriator as well, will thus be replaced by the mode of appropriation of the product based on the nature of the modern means of production themselves: on the one hand, direct social appropriation as a means of maintaining and extending production, and on the other direct individual appropriation as a means of existence and enjoyment.

By increasingly transforming the great majority of the population into proletarians, the capitalist mode of production creates the force which, under penalty of its own destruction, is compelled to accomplish this revolution. By increasingly driving towards the transformation of the vast socialised means of production into state property, it itself points the way to the accomplishment of this revolution. *The proletariat seizes state power and to begin with transforms the means of production into state property.* But it thus puts an end to itself as proletariat, it thus puts an end to all class differences and class antagonisms and thus also to the state as state. Moving in class antagonisms, society up to now had need of the state, that is, an organisation of the exploiting class at each period for the maintenance of its external conditions of production, that is, particularly for the forcible holding down of the exploited class in the conditions of oppression (slavery, villeinage or serfdom, wage labour) given by the existing mode of production. The state was the official representative of the whole of society, its concentration in a visible body, but it was so only in so far as it was the state of that class which in its time represented the whole of society: in antiquity, the state of the slave owning citizens, in the Middle Ages, of the feudal nobility, in our time, of the bourgeoisie. When ultimately it becomes the real representative of the whole of society, it renders itself superfluous. As soon as there is no social class to be held in subjection any longer, as soon as class domination and the struggle for individual existence based on the anarchy of production existing up to now are eliminated together with the collisions and excesses arising from them, there is nothing more to repress, nothing necessitating a special repressive force, a state. The first act in which the state really comes forward as the representative of the whole of society—the taking possession of the means of production in the name of society—is at the same time its last independent act as a state. The interference of the state power in social relations becomes superfluous in one sphere after another, and then dies away of itself. The government of persons is replaced by the administration of things and the direction of the processes of production. The state is not 'abolished', *it withers away*. It is by this that one must evaluate the phrase 'a free people's state' with respect both to its temporary agitational justification and to its ultimate scientific inadequacy, and it is by this that we must also evaluate the demand of the so called anarchists that the state should be abolished overnight.[6]

Since the historical emergence of the capitalist mode of production, the seizure of all the means of production by society has often been dreamed of, by individuals as well as by whole sects, more or less vaguely as an ideal of the future. But it could only become possible, it could only become a historical necessity, when the actual conditions for its realisation were present. Like every other social advance, it is becoming realisable not through the acquisition of the understanding that the existence of classes is in contradiction with justice, equality, etc, not through the mere will to abolish these classes, but through certain new economic conditions. The cleavage of society into an exploiting and an exploited class, a ruling and an oppressed class, was the necessary outcome of the previous low development of production. Society is necessarily divided into classes as long as the total social labour only yields a product but slightly exceeding what is necessary for the bare existence of all, as long as labour therefore claims all or almost all the time of the great majority of the members of society. Side by side with this great majority exclusively enthralled in toil, a class freed from direct productive labour is formed which manages the general business of society: the direction of labour, affairs of state, justice, science, art, and so forth. It is therefore the law of the division of labour which lies at the root of the division into classes. However, this does not mean that this division into classes was not established by violence and robbery, by deception and fraud, or that the ruling class, once in the saddle, has ever failed to strengthen its domination at the cost of the working class and to convert its direction of society into increased exploitation of the masses.

But if, upon this showing, division into classes has a certain historical justification, it does so only for a given period of time, for given social conditions. It was based on the insufficiency of production; it will be swept away by the full development of the modern productive forces. In fact the abolition of social classes presupposes a level of historical development at which the existence not merely of this or that particular ruling class but of any ruling class at all, and therefore of class distinction itself, has become an anachronism, is obsolete. It therefore presupposes that the development of production has reached a level at which the appropriation of the means of production and of the products, and consequently of political supremacy and of the monopoly of education and intellectual leadership by a special social class, has become not only superfluous but also a hindrance to development economically, politically and intellectually.

This point has now been reached. Its political and intellectual bankruptcy is hardly a secret any longer to the bourgeoisie itself, and its economic bankruptcy recurs regularly every ten years. In each crisis society is suffocated beneath the weight of its own productive forces and products of which it can make no use, and stands helpless in face of the absurd contradiction that the producers have nothing to consume because consumers are lacking. The expansive force of the means of production bursts asunder the bonds imposed upon them by the capitalist mode of production. Their release from these bonds is the sole prerequisite for an unbroken, ever more rapidly advancing development of the productive forces, and thus of a practically unlimited growth of production itself. Nor is this all. The social appropriation of the means of production puts an end not only to the current artificial restrictions on production, but also to the positive waste and devastation of productive forces and products which are now the inevitable concomitants of production and which reach their zenith in crises. Further, it sets free for the community at large a mass of means of production and products by putting an end to the senseless luxury and extravagance of the present ruling classes and their political representatives. The possibility of securing for every member of society, through social production, an existence which is not only perfectly adequate materially and which becomes daily richer, but also guarantees him the completely free development and exercise of his physical and mental faculties—this possibility is now present for the first time, but it *is present*.[7]

The seizure of the means of production by society eliminates commodity production and with it the domination of the product over the producer. The anarchy within social production is replaced by consciously planned organisation. The struggle for individual existence comes to an end. It is only at this point that man finally separates in a certain sense from the animal kingdom and that he passes from animal conditions of existence to really human ones. The conditions of existence environing and hitherto dominating humanity now pass under the dominion and control of humanity, which now for the first time becomes the real conscious master of nature, because and in so far as it becomes master of its own social organisation. The laws of man's own social activity, which have hitherto confronted him as extraneous laws of nature dominating him, will then be applied by man with full knowledge and hence be dominated by him. Man's own social organisation, which has hitherto confronted him as a process dictated by nature and history, now becomes a process resulting from his own voluntary action. The objective extraneous forces which have hitherto dominated history now pass under the control of man himself. It is only from this point that man will himself make his own history fully consciously, it is only from this point that the social causes he sets in motion will preponderantly and ever increasingly have the effects he wills. It is humanity's leap from the realm of necessity into the realm of freedom.

In conclusion, let us briefly sum up the course of our development:

1. Mediaeval Society: Small scale individual production. Means of production adapted to individual use, hence primitive, clumsy, petty, puny in effect. Production for immediate consumption, by the producer himself or by his feudal lord. Only where a surplus of production over this consumption occurs does this surplus get offered for sale and enter into exchange: production of commodities, therefore, only in its nascent state; but it already contains within itself, in embryo, *the anarchy in social production.*

2. Capitalist Revolution: Transformation of industry, at first by means of simple co-operation and manufacture. Concentration of the previously scattered means of production into large workshops, and consequently their transformation from individual into social means of production, a transformation which by and large does not affect the form of exchange. The old forms of appropriation remain in force. The *capitalist* appears: in his character as owner of the means of production he also appropriates the products and turns them into commodities. Production has become a social act; exchange and with it appropriation remain individual acts, the acts of individuals: *the social product is appropriated by the individual capitalist.* Fundamental contradiction, from which there arise all the contradictions in which present day society moves and which large scale industry brings to light.

A) Separation of the producer from the means of production. Condemnation of the worker to wage labour for life. *Antagonism of proletariat and bourgeoisie.*

B) Growing prominence and increasing effectiveness of the laws governing commodity production. Unbridled competitive struggle. *Contradiction between social organisation in the individual factory and social anarchy in production as a whole.*

C) On the one side, perfecting of machinery, which competition makes a compulsory commandment for each individual manufacturer, and which is equivalent to a constantly increasing displacement of

111

workers: *industrial reserve army*. On the other, unlimited expansion of production, likewise a compulsory law of competition for every manufacturer. On both sides, unheard of development of the productive forces, excess of supply over demand, overproduction, glutting of markets, crises every ten years, vicious circle: *here, superabundance of means of production and products—there, superabundance of workers* without employment and means of existence; but these two levers of production and of social well-being are unable to co-operate, because the capitalist form of production forbids the productive forces to function and the products to circulate unless they are first turned into capital—which their very superabundance prevents. The contradiction has grown into an absurdity: *the mode of production rebels against the form of exchange*. The bourgeoisie is convicted of incapacity to manage its own social productive forces any further.

D) Partial recognition of the social character of the productive forces imposed on the capitalists themselves. Appropriation of the large production and communication organisations, first by *joint stock companies*, later by trusts, then by the *state*. The bourgeoisie proves itself a superfluous class; all its social functions are now performed by salaried employees.

3. Proletarian Revolution, solution of the contradictions: the proletariat seizes the public power and by virtue of this power transforms the social means of production, which are slipping from the hands of the bourgeoisie, into public property. By this act, the proletariat frees the means of production from their previous character as capital, and gives their social character complete freedom to assert

112

itself. Social production according to a predetermined plan now becomes possible. The development of production makes the further existence of different social classes an anachronism. In proportion as the anarchy of social production vanishes, the political authority of the state dies away. Men, at last masters of their own mode of social organisation, consequently become at the same time masters of nature, masters of themselves—free.

To accomplish this world-emancipating act is the historical mission of the modern proletariat. To grasp the historical conditions of this act and therefore its very nature, and thus to bring the conditions and character of its own action to the consciousness of the class that is destined to act, the class that is now oppressed—this is the task of scientific socialism, the theoretical expression of the proletarian movement.

Notes

⬤Notes prefixed 'E' were added by Engels to his original text. The rest are those of the editors of this edition.

Foreword to the first French edition

1. Frederick Engels, *Anti-Dühring. Herr Eugen Dühring's Revolution in Science*.
2. The *Deutsch-Französische Jahbücher* (*German-French Yearbooks*) was a German publication edited by Marx and Arnold Ruge. Only one issue ever came out, a double number in February 1844.
3. The Communist Association of German Workers was founded by Marx and Engels in Brussels in August 1847.
    The Deutsche-Brüsseler-Zeitung (*German Brussels Gazette*) came under the influence of Marx and Engels in late 1847 and eventually became a paper of the Communist League.
4. *Neue Reinische Zeitung* (*New Rhine Gazette*) was published daily in Cologne between 1 June 1848 and 19 May 1849 and represented the

working class wing of the revolutionary movement. Marx was editor in chief.

5. *Neue Reinische Zeitung. Politisch-ökonomische Revue (New Rhine Gazette. Political and Economic Review)* was the brain-child of Marx and Engels and published in the course of 1850 as the journal of the Communist League.

6. *Der Volksstaat (The People's State)* was the main publication of the German Social Democratic Workers Party, published between 2 October 1869 and 29 September 1876, after which it was fused with the *Neue Sozialdemokrat (New Social Democrat)* to form *Vorwärts (Forward)*.

Preface to the first German edition

1. *Der Sozialdemokrat (The Social Democrat)* was the weekly paper of the German Social Democratic Party, published abroad during the period of the Anti Socialist Laws between 1879 and 1890.

2. Von Sybel and Treitschke were German establishment historians.

3. **E** 'In Germany' is a slip of the pen. It should read 'among Germans'. For the developed economic and political conditions of England and France were as indispensible for the genesis of scientific socialism as was German dialectics. The economic and political stage of development of Germany, which at the beginnings of the 'forties was much more backward than it is today, could at most produce caricatures of socialism (cf. *The Communist Manifesto*, Chapter III, Section I, c. 'German or "True" Socialism'). Only by subjecting the conditions

produced in England and France to German
dialectical criticism could a genuine result be
achieved. From this angle, therefore, scientific
socialism is not *exclusively* a German product but
equally an international one. [This was added by
Engels to the 1883 German edition].

Introduction to the first English edition

1. Eugen Dühring, *A Course in Philosophy*, Leipzig
    1875; *A Course in Political and Social Economy*,
    2nd edn., Leipzig 1876; *A Critical History of
    Political Economy and Socialism*, 2nd edn.,
    Berlin 1875.
2. Omitted from this edition.
3. Nominalism was a mediaeval philosophy which
    held that universal and collective terms are
    merely names of individual objects.
4. Anaxagoras, through his homoiomeriae, believed
    in matter being constituted from basic particles.
5. E 'Qual' is a philosophical play upon words.
    Qual literally means torture, a pain which drives
    to action of some kind; at the same time the
    mystic Böhme puts into the German word
    something of the meaning of the Latin *qualitas*;
    'qual' was the activating principle arising from,
    and promoting in its turn, the spontaneous
    development of the thing, relation or person
    subject to it, in contradistinction to the pain
    inflicted from without.
6. The difference between theism and deism is that
    the first is a belief in a personal god, the second
    in an impersonal one.
    Engels added here a reference to Marx and

Engels, *Die Heillege Familie* (The Holy Family), Frankfurt am Main, 1845, pp. 201-4.

7. **E** And even in business matters, the conceit of national chauvinism is but a sorry advisor. Up to quite recently, the average English manufacturer considered it derogatory for an Englishman to speak any language but his own, and felt rather proud than otherwise of the fact that 'poor devils' of foreigners settled in England and took off his hands the trouble of disposing of his products abroad. He never noticed that these foreigners, mostly Germans, thus got command of a very large part of British foreign trade, imports and exports, and that the direct foreign trade of Englishmen became limited, almost entirely, to the colonies, China, the United States and South America. Nor did he notice that these Germans traded with other Germans abroad, who gradually organised a complete network of commercial colonies all over the world. But when Germany, about 40 years ago, seriously began manufacturing for export, this network served her admirably in her transformation, in so short a time, from a corn exporting into a first rate manufacturing country. Then, about ten years ago, the British manufacturer got frightened, and asked his ambassadors and consuls how it was that he could no longer keep his customers together, the unanimous answer was: (1) You don't learn your customer's language but expect him to speak your own; (2) You don't even try to suit your customer's wants, habits and tastes, but expect him to conform to your English ones.

8. By Katheder Socialism Engels is referring to academics who claim to be socialists, but denounce working class struggle. 'Katheder' is the German word for university chair. Today we would say 'armchair'.

Chapter 1

1.   **E** This is the passage on the French Revolution: 'The thought, the concept of right, *all at once* asserted itself, and against this the old scaffolding of wrong could make no stand. In this conception of right, therefore, a constitution has now been established, and henceforth everything must be based on this. Ever since the sun has been in the firmament and the planets have circled round it, the sight had never been seen of man standing on his head—ie on thought—and building reality out of this image. Anaxagoras was the first to say that nous, reason, rules the world; but now, for the first time, man had come to recognise that the Idea must rule mental reality. And this was a *magnificent sunrise. All thinking beings have joined in celebrating this epoch. A sublime emotion* prevailed at that time, *an enthusiasm to reason sent a thrill through the world*, as if the reconciliation of the divine with the profane had only now come about.' (Hegel, *Philosophy of History*, German edition, 1840, p. 535). Is it not high time to set the Anti Socialist Law in action against these teachings of the late Professor which are so subversive and such a public danger? [Italics in the last three sentences of the quote from Hegel are Engels'].

2.   Münzer (around 1490-1525) was a leader and ideologist of the radical peasant-plebeian wing during the Reformation and the Peasants' War. The Levellers stood on the extreme left wing of the English Revolution.

   Babeuf (1760-97) was a utopian communist and the theorist and leader of the 'Conspiracy of Equals'.

3.   *Lettres d'un habitant de Genève à ses*

contemporains (*Letters of a Resident of Geneva to His Contemporaries*) is Saint-Simon's first work; it was written in Geneva in 1802 and published anonymously in Paris in 1803.

The first work of importance by Charles Fourier was *Théorie des quatre mouvements et des destinées générales* (*Theory of the Four Movements and Destinies in General*), written early in the 19th century and published anonymously in Lyons in 1808.

New Lanark—a cotton mill with a workers' settlement in Scotland—was founded in the early 1780s.

4.   'Lettres d'un habitant de Genève à ses contemporains' in *Œuvres de Claude-Henri de Saint-Simon*, Editions Anthropos, Paris 1966, Vol. I, Book I, pp. 41-2, 55.

5.   The eighth letter in the series: 'Lettres de Henri Saint-Simon à un Américain', Ibid., Vol. I, Book II, p. 186.

6.   Engels is referring to the two pamphlets co-authored by Saint-Simon and A Thierry: 'De la réorganisation de la société Européenne...' and 'Opinion sur les mesures à prendre contre la coalition de 1815'. The first was written in October 1814, the second in May 1815. Ibid., Vol. I, Book I, pp. 153-218 and Vol. VI, pp. 353-79.

7.   See Fourier's statement in his first book, *Théorie des quatre mouvements*: 'As a general thesis, social progress and changes in a period take place by reason of the progress of women towards freedom, and the decay of the social system takes place by reason of the decrease in women's freedom.' From this he draws the following conclusion: 'The extension of the rights of women is the basic principle of all social progress.' (Fourier, *Textes choisis*, edited by F Armand, Editions Sociales. Paris 1953, p. 124.)

8. Ibid., pp. 64-5, 70.

9. Ibid., pp. 95, 105. For the 'vicious circle' of civilisation, see pp. 104, 129-30.

10. Ibid., pp. 66-7.

11. See AL Morton, *The Life and Ideas of Robert Owen*, London 1962, p. 80.

12. **E** From 'The Revolution in the Mind and Practice of the Human Race', a memorial addressed to all the 'red Republicans, Communists and Socialists of Europe', and sent to the provisional government of France, 1848, and also, 'to Queen Victoria and her responsible advisers'.

13. Robert Owen, 'Report of the Proceedings at the Several Public Meetings, Held in Dublin... on the 18th March, 12th April, 19th April and 3rd May', Dublin 1823.

14. An Act, introduced on Owen's initiative in June 1815, was passed by Parliament in July 1819 after it had been watered down. The Act regulating labour at cotton mills banned the employment of children under nine and limited the working day to 12 hours for people under 16. Since Owen's proposal for paid inspectors was defeated, the Act became a dead letter.

15. In October 1833 Owen presided over a congress of co-operative societies and trade unions in London, which led to the formation of the Grand National Consolidated Trades Union in February 1834.

16. Equitable Labour Exchange Bazaars were founded by workers' co-operatives in various parts of England; Owen opened the National Equitable Labour Exchange Bazaar in London in September 1832 and it existed until mid-1834. Proudhon made an attempt to organise the Banque du Peuple in Paris in January 1849. It existed, on paper, for about two months.

Chapter 2

1. For an English translation of *Le Neveu de Rameau*, see Diderot, *Rameau's Nephew* and *D'Alembert's Dream*, Harmondsworth 1966; for an English translation of *Discourse on the Origin of Inequality Among Men*, see Rousseau, *The Social Contract and Discourses*.
2. The Alexandrian period of science dates from the third century BC. Its name derives from the Egyptian port of Alexandria, which was a major centre of international trade.

Chapter 3.

1. **E** There is no need to explain here that, even if the form of appropriation remains the same, the character of the appropriation is just as much revolutionised as production by the process described above. Of course two very different kinds of appropriation are involved in whether I appropriate my own product or that of another person. It may be noted in passing that wage labour, in which the whole capitalist mode of production is to be already found in embryo, is very ancient; in a sporadic, scattered form it existed for centuries alongside slave labour. But the embryo could develop into the capitalist mode of production only when the necessary historical preconditions had been established.
2. *The Condition of the Working Class in England*, p. 109 [German Edition]. [This reference noted by Engels.] Marx and Engels, *On Britain*,

Moscow 1954, p. 119.

3.   See Marx, *Capital*, Moscow 1961, Vol. 1, pp. 408, 435-6, 462, 487.

4.   Ibid., p. 645, Engels' italics.

5.   **E** I say is constrained to.
For it is only when the means of production or communication have actually outgrown direction by joint stock companies and therefore their nationalisation has become economically inevitable—it is only then that this nationalisation, even when carried out by the state of today, represents an economic advance, the attainment of another preliminary step towards the seizure of all the productive forces by society itself. But since Bismarck became keen on nationalising, a certain spurious socialism has recently made its appearance—here and there even degenerating into a kind of flunkeyism—which without more ado declares all nationalisation, even the Bismarckian kind, to be socialistic. To be sure, if the nationalisation of the tobacco trade were socialistic, Napoleon and Metternich would rank among the founders of socialism. If the Belgian state, for quite ordinary political and financial reasons, constructed its own main railway lines, if Bismarck, without any economic compulsion, nationalised the main Prussian railway lines simply in order to be better able to organise and use them in face of war, in order to train the railway officials as the government's voting cattle, and especially in order to secure a new source of revenue independent of parliamentary votes, such actions were in no sense socialistic measures, whether direct or indirect, conscious or unconscious. Otherwise, the Royal Maritime Company, the Royal Porcelain Manufacture, and even the regimental tailors in the army would be socialist institutions, or even, as was seriously proposed

by a sly dog in the 'thirties, during the reign of
Frederick William III, the nationalisation of
the—brothels.

6. A 'free people's state': this slogan is criticised in
Marx's *Critique of the Gotha Programme,* Peking
1972, pp. 26-9, Engels' letter to Bebel of March
18-28, 1875 (ibid., pp. 42-3), and Lenin's *The
State and Revolution*, Peking 1970,
pp. 21-2, 76-9.

7. E A few figures may give an approximate idea of
the enormous expansive force of the modern
means of production even under the weight of
capitalism. According to Giffen's latest
estimates, [Robert Giffen, 'Recent
Accumulations of Capital in the United
Kingdom', *Journal of the Statistical Society*,
London, Vol. 16, 1878.] the total wealth of Great
Britain and Ireland was, in round figures:
1814 £2,200,000,000
1865 £6,100,000,000
1875 £8,500,000,000
As for the squandering of means of production
and products resulting from crises, the total loss
to the German iron industry alone in the last
crash was estimated at 455,000,000 marks
[£22,750,000] at the Second German Industrial
Congress (Berlin, 21 February 1878).

Further reading

THIS BOOK is a basic introduction to socialism.
Hopefully most readers will want to learn a lot
more. In particular, how do the ideas of Engels
and Marx fit with the world of today?

The list of titles below is provided as
suggestions. You might want to follow up a
particular topic, or you might want to dip into a bit
of everything. .

Those titles marked '#' are short pamphlets.
Any of this list can be obtained from your local
socialist bookstall, or from Bookmarks (phone
081-802 6145).

Other introductions to socialism

How Marxism works • Chris Harman
Can socialism come through parliament?# • Pat
Stack
The struggle for workers' power# • Charlie
Kimber
Why we need a revolutionary party# • Lindsey
German
The communist manifesto# • Marx and Engels

Arguments for revolutionary socialism • John
Molyneux
The revolutionary ideas of Karl Marx • Alex
Callinicos
What is the real Marxist tradition? • John
Molyneux
Marxism and the party • John Molyneux

Socialist education packs

1. *Marxism and the modern world#*
4. *Basic ideas of Marxist economics#*
5. *Women's liberation and the class struggle#*
6. *What we mean by the 'isms'#*
7. *Marxism and the national question#*

Marxist economics and the crisis

Where is capitalism going? (ISJ 58) • Chris
Harman
Wage labour and capital# • Marx
Wages, price and profit# • Marx
Why the world economy is in crisis# • Peter Green
Man's worldly goods • Leo Huberman

The working class movement in Britain

Days of Hope: The General Strike of 1926# •
Duncan Hallas and Chris Harman
Socialism and the Labour Party# • Duncan
Blackie

The changing working class • Alex Callinicos and Chris Harman
1919: Britain on the brink of revolution • Chanie Rosenberg
The making of the English working class • EP Thompson
Marxism and trade union struggle: the General Strike of 1926 • Tony Cliff and Donny Gluckstein
The Labour Party: a Marxist history • Tony Cliff and Donny Gluckstein

The international working class movement

Homage to Catalonia • George Orwell
The Comintern • Duncan Hallas.
The lost revolution: Germany 1918-23 • Chris Harman
Teamster rebellion • Farrell Dobbs
Nicaragua: What went wrong? • Mike Gonzalez
South Africa between apartheid and capitalism • Alex Callinicos
Israel: the hijack state • John Rose
Zionism: false Messiah • Nathan Weinstock

Imperialism, the national question and the Third World

Hope amidst the horror: the socialist answer to world hunger# • Mark O'Brien
Deflected permanent revolution# • Tony Cliff
Imperialism, highest stage of capitalism • Lenin

The rights of nations to self determination • Lenin
Permanent Revolution • Leon Trotsky

Women's liberation, racism and Ireland

The struggle for women's liberation# • Elane Heffernan
Origins of the family, private property and the state • Engels
Sex, class and socialism • Lindsey German
Women workers and the trade unions • Sara Boston
Malcolm X. Socialism and Black Nationalism • Kevin Ovenden
The fight against racism# • Alex Callinicos
Racism, resistance and revolution • Peter Alexander
Staying power: black people in Britain • Peter Fryer
Ireland: why the troops must get out# • Chris Bambery
Ireland's permanent revolution • Chris Bambery
Labour in Irish History • James Connolly

BOOKMARKS
265 Seven Sisters Road, London N4 2DE
PO Box 16085, Chicago, Il, 60616
GPO Box 1473N, Melbourne, 3001